跨境电商客户服务与管理

徐 娜 主编

北京理工大学出版社
BEIJING INSTITUTE OF TECHNOLOGY PRESS

版权专有　侵权必究

图书在版编目（CIP）数据

跨境电商客户服务与管理／徐娜主编．—北京：北京理工大学出版社，2019.2（2023.8重印）
ISBN 978 – 7 – 5682 – 6391 – 7

Ⅰ.①跨…　Ⅱ.①徐…　Ⅲ.①电子商务 – 商业服务 – 高等学校 – 教材②电子商务 – 运营管理 – 高等学校 – 教材　Ⅳ.①F713.365

中国版本图书馆 CIP 数据核字（2018）第 224003 号

出版发行／北京理工大学出版社有限责任公司	
社　　址／北京市海淀区中关村南大街 5 号	
邮　　编／100081	
电　　话／（010）68914775（总编室）	
（010）82562903（教材售后服务热线）	
（010）68944723（其他图书服务热线）	
网　　址／http://www.bitpress.com.cn	
经　　销／全国各地新华书店	
印　　刷／廊坊市印艺阁数字科技有限公司	
开　　本／787 毫米 × 1092 毫米　1/16	
印　　张／8.25	责任编辑／梁铜华
字　　数／191 千字	文案编辑／梁铜华
版　　次／2019 年 2 月第 1 版　2023 年 8 月第 3 次印刷	责任校对／杜　枝
定　　价／39.00 元	责任印制／施胜娟

图书出现印装质量问题，请拨打售后服务热线，本社负责调换

编 委

主　编：徐　娜
副主编：陶　琳
参　编：张鸿飞　马小微　王春娟　李　峥

序

前　言

　　电子商务作为我国领跑于世界的商业模式，发展速度快，渗透领域广，在企业中的应用领先于高等教育发展，其技术手段更新频繁。而跨境电子商务对国际贸易运作方式、贸易链环节产生了革命性、实质性的影响。我国政府高度重视跨境电商的发展，将其视为新时期中国经济发展的引擎、产业转型的新业态和对外开放的新窗口，接连进行政策创新，支持跨境电商的发展。

　　随着近两年跨境电商的持续火爆，新的岗位需求日益凸显——跨境电商客服专员。而跨境电商的客户服务与以淘宝为代表的国内电商客户服务、传统大宗商品国际贸易的客户服务都有着很大的区别。跨境电商服务的对象具有全球化、碎片化和在线化的特点，这让客户的需求和标准变得多层次；海外客户的电商消费模式更多是通过页面描述、站内信的方式沟通交流，因为价值观、宗教信仰的区别，万一产生售后问题，在退货成本、沟通精力、运营风险等方面都会使卖家面临很大的考验。这就需要运营跨境电商的卖家客服人员熟悉跨境平台规则，深入了解客户需求，抓住客户的购物心理，搜寻网罗潜在目标客户，掌握售前、售中、售后不同阶段的服务技巧，识别防范交易风险等。因此，本教材特别为跨境客服岗位从业人员进行相关专业性学习而设计，按照企业工作岗位的专业技能与工作任务甄选教材内容。

　　跨境电商对于高等教育是新生事物，是近一年各高等院校紧随人才需求纷纷开设的专业方向，本书按照主流跨境电商平台的功能应用及企业对跨境商务运营人才的培养要求和相关工作岗位的专业技能而设计，以亚马逊、速卖通等主流跨境平台店铺为背景，旨在体现工学结合教学模式的特色，培养学生跨境电子商务实操技能。本书的编写思路是以跨境电商客户服务岗位实际工作任务为导向，以工作流程为主线，将内容分为产品详情页、公共信息服务、售前咨询、发货服务、售后客服、促销活动、社交媒体推广、客户关系管理八大情境。在编写过程中，始终贯穿以跨境电商客服岗位实践技能为主体的结构，同时突出工作语言环境；设计了以学生为中心的项目，推出了以任务为引领的教学模式。每章包括学习目标、项目背景、新手指南、任务实施、跨境电商中英术语对照五大板块，并根据不同项目内容辅以语言训练、案例解析、知识加油站等内容。

　　本书由徐娜老师主持编写，负责全书的整体设计和统稿。项目一由张鸿飞老师编写，项目二、六由陶琳老师编写，项目五、八由徐娜老师编写，项目四由王春娟老师编写，项目七由马小微老师编写，项目三由李峥老师编写。

　　本书可作为高等院校电子商务、商务英语、国际贸易、国际商务、市场营销、物流管理等专业的教学用书，也可供中职、高职、本科衔接院校在教学时作为参考，还可作为其他专业学生和电商企业运营、客服人员的培训教材。

　　本书在编写过程中采撷了大量相关资料、网络资料和专家学者的成果，恕不能一一列出。由于编者水平有限、时间匆忙等因素，难免有疏漏之处，望读者批评指正。

编　者

目 录
Contents

Project 1　Product Listing（产品详情页） ·· (1)
　　Learning Aims（学习目标） ·· (1)
　　Lead-in Situation（项目背景） ·· (1)
　　Green-hand Guide（新手指南） ·· (1)
　　Mission Implementation（任务实施） ·· (2)
　　Cross-border E-commerce English-Chinese Vocabulary（跨境电商英汉术语对照） ······ (14)

Project 2　Commonplace Services（公共信息） ································ (17)
　　Learning Aims（学习目标） ·· (17)
　　Lead-in Situation（项目背景） ·· (17)
　　Green-hand Guide（新手指南） ·· (17)
　　Mission Implementation（任务实施） ·· (25)
　　Cross-border E-commerce English-Chinese Vocabulary（跨境电商英汉术语对照） ······ (30)

Project 3　Pre-sale Consulting（售前咨询） ···································· (32)
　　Learning Aims（学习目标） ·· (32)
　　Lead-in Situation（项目背景） ·· (32)
　　Green-hand Guide（新手指南） ·· (32)
　　Mission Implementation（任务实施） ·· (37)
　　Cross-border E-commerce English-Chinese Vocabulary（跨境电商英汉术语对照） ······ (47)

Project 4　Delivery Service（发货服务） ·· (50)
　　Learning Aims（学习目标） ·· (50)
　　Lead-in Situation（项目背景） ·· (50)
　　Green-hand Guide（新手指南） ·· (50)
　　Mission Implementation（任务实施） ·· (56)

Cross-border E-commerce English-Chinese Vocabulary（跨境电商英汉术语对照）…… (62)

Project 5　After-sale Service（售后客服）………………………………………… (63)
　　Learning Aims（学习目标）……………………………………………………… (63)
　　Lead-in Situation（项目背景）…………………………………………………… (63)
　　Cross-border E-commerce Platform Rules（跨境电商平台规则）…………… (63)
　　Green-hand Guide（新手指南）………………………………………………… (69)
　　Mission Implementation（任务实施）…………………………………………… (74)
　　Cross-border E-commerce English-Chinese Vocabulary（跨境电商英汉术语对照）…… (80)

Project 6　Sales Promotion（促销活动）……………………………………………… (83)
　　Learning Aims（学习目标）……………………………………………………… (83)
　　Lead-in Situation（项目背景）…………………………………………………… (83)
　　Cross-border E-commerce Platform Sales Promotion Classification（跨境电商平台
　　促销活动分类）…………………………………………………………………… (83)
　　Green-hand Guide（新手指南）………………………………………………… (84)
　　Mission Implementation（任务实施）…………………………………………… (94)
　　Cross-border E-commerce English-Chinese Vocabulary（跨境电商英汉术语对照）… (100)

Project 7　SNS Marketing（社交媒体推广）……………………………………… (101)
　　Learning Aims（学习目标）……………………………………………………… (101)
　　Lead-in Situation（项目背景）…………………………………………………… (101)
　　Green-hand Guide（新手指南）………………………………………………… (103)
　　Mission Implementation（任务实施）…………………………………………… (112)
　　Cross-border E-commerce English-Chinese Vocabulary（跨境电商英汉术语对照）… (113)

Project 8　Customer Relationship Management（客户关系管理）……………… (115)
　　Learning Aims（学习目标）……………………………………………………… (115)
　　Lead-in Situation（项目背景）…………………………………………………… (115)
　　Green-hand Guide（新手指南）………………………………………………… (115)
　　Mission Implementation（任务实施）…………………………………………… (119)
　　Cross-border E-commerce English-Chinese Vocabulary（跨境电商英汉术语对照）… (122)

Project 1

Product Listing（产品详情页）

Learning Aims（学习目标）

From learning this chapter, students will have a good understanding of making a product listing.
1. Know the special terms often used in cross-border e-commerce.
2. Describe products in smooth English.
3. Summarize bullet points of products precisely in English.
4. Grasp basic knowledge of exposure rate.

Lead-in Situation（项目背景）

应届高职毕业生小张成功被小熊贸易公司录取，并聘用为跨境电商亚马逊平台客服专员。第一天她被主管安排先登录亚马逊官网浏览熟悉公司经营的产品。作为职场菜鸟，小张知道自己必须从头学起，作为客服专员，只有详细了解了产品详情页的设计与描述，才能与客户更加高效、顺畅地沟通。

Green-hand Guide（新手指南）

无论是初次涉及电商市场的新买家还是经验丰富的老买家，没有一个人会在不参考任何产品详情页的情况下就进行购物。什么是产品详情页呢？它是展示商品详细信息的一个页面，承载着电商平台的大部分流量和订单的入口。一个吸引人的产品详情页就像专卖店里一名好的推销员一样，面对各式各样的客户，或是用语言打动消费者，或是用视觉特效传达商品的优点，将潜在的客户群变为实在的消费者。图1-1就是亚马逊平台一个简单的产品详情页截图。

1-1 产品发布

制作产品详情页一般要遵循两个基本点和六个原则。

两个基本点：一是把所有的客户都当成非专业人士；二是寻找产品的价值点而非促销点。

1-2 标题与关键词

六个原则：
1. 三秒原则：三秒钟必须引起客户的注意力。
2. 前三屏原则：前三屏决定客户是否想购买商品。
3. 讲故事原则：情感营销引起买家的共鸣。
4. 一句话原则：用一句话提炼产品卖点。

图1-1 亚马逊平台产品详情页示例

5. 重复性原则：商品卖点只需要一个且要不停地告诉客户。
6. 回答原则：诉求利益因素给她一个购买的理由。

Mission Implementation（任务实施）

了解了上述基本概念和原则之后，徐姐开始了对小张的培训。"小张，早晨好！我是徐姐，负责对你进行一些简单的岗前培训。我们的培训一共有三项任务，主要是为了让你了解和熟悉产品详情页的设计思路和优化技巧，未来更好地为客户提供服务。我们马上开始培训吧！"

Task 1　Explaining Your Product Listing（产品详情页详解）

打开一个亚马逊主站产品详情页链接 http://www.amazon.com/dp/B00TQCLY8K，会看到页面（图1-2）。

图1-2 产品详情页内容布局（1）

对应图 1-2 中标记的数字，各个栏目的内容如表 1-1 所示。

表 1-1 产品详情页内容

序号	类别	序号	类别
1	产品类目	6	购物车
2	产品品牌	7	其他卖家信息
3	卖家和配送方式	8	产品描述
4	产品特性要点（卖点）	9	产品 ASIN 码
5	跟踪卖家	10	产品在类目中的排名

Notes 说明

（1）针对序号 5 的说明：在亚马逊平台，如果 A 卖家上架了一件商品，B 卖家正好有同品牌、同款式（型号）的商品也准备上架，那么 B 卖家可以去 A 卖家的商品详情页右侧寻找 "Have one to sell?"，然后点击 "Sell on Amazon（跟卖）"。那么，当买家浏览 A 卖家的商品时，点击第 5 项 "New from $4.50"，B 卖家的商品会作为 "跟卖商品" 显示出来。

（2）针对序号 9 的说明：产品的 ASIN 码，即 Amazon Standard Identification Number（亚马逊标准产品识别码），是由字母和数字组成的十位数码，由亚马逊平台自动分配给每一种商品，可通过输入 ASIN 码直接搜索商品。ASIN 码还会显示在产品链接中，例如 "B00TQCLY8K" 就是案例介绍产品的 ASIN 码。

徐姐："下面我将随机选择一个页面，请你分别标出 10 个类别的位置。"

Activity　Highlight the 10 special terms in Figure 1-3（标出图 1-3 中 10 项内容位置）.

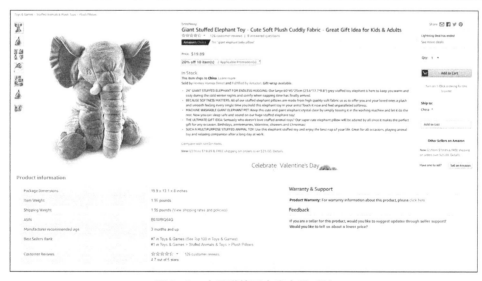

图 1-3 产品详情页内容布局（2）

Task 2　Describing Your Product Listing（产品详情页撰写）

第二个任务主要涉及产品详情页的撰写和细化。一般情况下，人们都会被详细的商品信息所吸引。精准、翔实、可靠的商品信息能够大幅提升消费者的购买兴趣，促成潜在消费者向事实消费者的转化。如何将一样商品描述得准确、详细、生动是这个任务中我们要解决的问题，要解决这个问题需要从四个部分入手。

Activity 1　Product title（产品标题）.

产品标题作为买家对产品的第一印象来源，直接决定着产品链接的点击率。想撰写出一条吸引人的产品标题，就必须注意表 1-2 所示的几点。

表 1-2　产品标题撰写注意事项

Dos 可以做	Don'ts 禁止做
必须从消费者角度出发	不能堆叠形容词
尽量包含产品核心指标和信息	不能超过 140 个字符
尽量包含和产品有关的流行词或短语	不能出现法律法规限制和禁止使用的词语

Example（案例分析）

根据产品的具体情况撰写一条产品标题。

产品类型：牛仔裤

产品品牌：Lee

产品款式：男式修身款

使用程度：二手

材　　质：全棉

颜　　色：蓝色、棕色、黑色

产　　地：越南

发货方式：代理商发货

特别说明：限量款

撰写过程：使用程度＋产品类型＋产品款式＋品牌＋特别说明＋材质＋颜色＋产地＋发货方式

答　　案：Second-hand Men's Slim Jeans Limited Edition of Lee 100% Cotton Three Colors Made in Vietnam Lot Drop Shipping

翻　　译：二手男式修身牛仔裤，Lee 品牌限量款，全棉材质，三种颜色可供选择，越南生产，代理商发货

Notes（解析）

如何才能撰写一条吸引人的产品标题？

1. 产品标题中必须写清产品品牌。
2. 产品标题中必须写清产品特性。
3. 产品标题中尽量写清产品产地。
4. 产品标题中不要出现宽泛的形容词，例如：美丽、大方、严肃等。
5. 产品标题中不要出现标点符号、星号、拟声词、叹词等。
6. 产品标题中不要出现任何缩写词。

徐姐："小张，你练习一下根据产品的信息来撰写产品标题。"

Practice（练习）：**Write a product title according to the following details**（根据产品详情撰写产品标题）.

产品类型：电脑套装
产品品牌：戴尔
产品款式：商用台式机
使用程度：全新
产品配置：Windows 10 家用操作系统，键盘，鼠标，17 英寸① LCD 显示器
产　　地：中国香港
特别说明：官方认证翻新机
撰写过程：使用程度 + 产品品牌 + 产品款式 + 产品类型 + 产品配置 + 产地 + 特别说明
答　　案：_____
　　　　　_____
翻　　译：_____
　　　　　_____

Activity 2　Key words（关键词）.

如果一件产品多次被不同消费者搜索到，就说明它的产品详情页内容中一定包含了多角度的"关键词"，我们要学习的内容就是关键词的选择。

消费者进行网络购物时大部分情况下只需要在搜索栏中输入心仪产品的名称，搜索引擎就会自动检索出相关产品。简单来说，关键词就是产品本身是什么。例如：消费者想购买女孩子的裙子，只需要输入"girl dress"，就会出现各式裙子供消费者选择。这种通过输入关键词来检索产品的方式被称为关键词搜索。

关键词搜索最早被广泛应用于图书馆管理。通过提取和概括包含文献内容的关键词来整理和归档各类书籍、论文和报告等。在电子商务空前繁荣的今天，各大网络购物平台争相将自身的搜索引擎升级为关键词搜索引擎。通过提取产品的特征来确定关键词。当消费者搜索这一关键词时，包含相同关键词的所有产品都将被一一列出。因此，关键词的选择决定着卖家的产品能否顺利被消费者搜索到。

在选择关键词的过程中，卖家必须遵循两个原则：变化原则（Variety Rule）和长尾原则（Long Tail Rule）。

变化原则主要从消费者角度出发，充分考虑消费者的搜索习惯，强调在选择关键词的时候可以使用同义词、替代词、缩写词等词语。长尾原则主要从卖家角度出发，强调在选择关键词的时候应使用个性化的、精准化的词语。这一方面可以迅速吸引消费者，另一方面也可以快速锁定潜在客户，避免各卖家之间的过度竞争。

Notes（解析）

如何选择出与众不同的关键词呢？

1. 使用产品品牌、认证商标或者特殊缩写。
2. 使用搜索度高的同义词或者替代词替换产品名称。
3. 使用自制的长尾词（精细化描述产品的个性化属性），不要复制粘贴网络流行词。

---

① 1 英寸 = 2.54 厘米。

徐姐:"卖家可能会要求我们帮助判断他们选择的关键词是否有效,是否吸引潜在消费者。我们可以借助关键词搜索引擎来验证。下面我就介绍一款最常用的关键词搜索软件Sonar(声呐)的用法。"

Example(案例分析）

Sonar 是一款免费的亚马逊关键词搜索调研软件,由 Sellics 公司推出,综合亚马逊6个平台站点数据(美国、英国、法国、意大利、西班牙和德国),允许用户搜索7 400多万个关键词。Sonar 能帮助卖家提高关键词排名并且优化付费广告效果。在 Sonar 网站,卖家可进行三种不同的关键词搜索(Keyword/Extended/ASIN)。

第一种是 Keyword(常规关键词)搜索。卖家输入产品名称,Sonar 会检索出一系列热搜关键词。比如,输入"golf balls",Sonar 会给卖家推荐"practice golf balls""titleist golf balls""used golf balls"等(图1-4)。

图1-4 Sonar 搜索结果示例(1)

第二种是 Extended(基于关键词)搜索,同时添加同义词、替代词和相关词条。比如,输入"golf balls",推荐的关键词有"golf""golf accessories""golf tees"等(图1-5)。

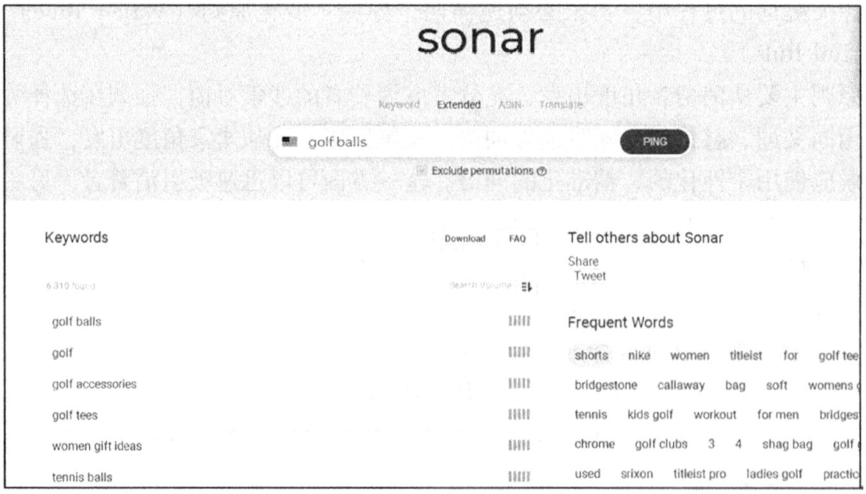

图1-5 Sonar 搜索结果示例(2)

第三种是 ASIN 搜索。卖家只需输入产品 ASIN 编号，就可搜索出热门关键词。这意味着卖家能看到、效仿甚至优化竞争对手正在使用的关键词。在 Sonar 中输入"B01MUEUWSS"，则软件搜索出亚马逊网站上与"B01MUEUWSS"编码相对应的产品最热门产品是"titleist golf balls""titleist pro v1 golf balls""titleist pro v1"。最热门关键词显示在页面右下方，有"golf""titleist""golf balls""v1""pro""ball"（图 1-6）。

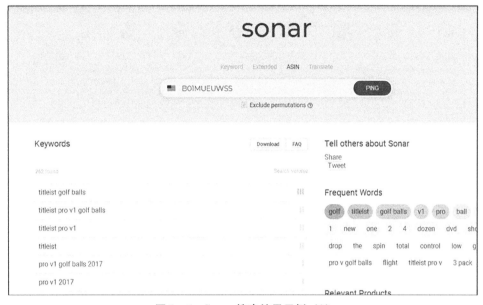

图 1-6 Sonar 搜索结果示例（3）

Practice（练习）：**Find out your interested product and search lts key words on Sonar**（找出你感兴趣的商品并用 **Sonar** 搜索关键词）.

Activity 3　Bullet points（产品卖点）.

产品卖点是对产品信息的高度提炼和概括，一般分为自身卖点和差异化卖点。自身卖点主要包括产品本身的性能、外观、功能等；差异化卖点则偏重于体现产品本身区别于其他同类产品的特性和优势，可以从设计、功能（功效）、配套服务等方面入手。

亚马逊平台的产品卖点一般位于产品标题（Product Title）下方，包括四至五个要点：每个要点首字母大写；可使用短语、句子或者短语+句子的形式；尽量使用同一语言结构；一条卖点不能超过 100 个字符，全部卖点不能超过 500 个字符；不能有特殊字符。

以亚马逊平台某电子秤产品截图（图 1-7）为例，产品卖点一般位于产品标题（Product Title）下方，包括 4~5 个要点描述，每个要点描述的首字母大写；可使用短语、句子或者短语+句子的形式；尽量使用同一语言结构；一条卖点不能超过 100 个字符，全部卖点不能超过 500 个字符；不能有特殊字符。

Notes（解析）

如何准确提炼产品卖点？

1. 对产品进行初步定位：概念前卫、设计新颖、包装美观的产品，在后续的卖点提炼中易开展较为平实的叙述；功能普通、基本无设计感、包装简陋的产品，在后续的卖点提炼中应尽量搜集信息，提炼优点，为差异化营销做充分准备。

2. 从消费者角度出发，多角度、全方位进行提炼。

图1-7 电子秤产品卖点

3. 从对同类产品的提问、评价、客服、运输等环节提炼卖点（从好评中提炼自身卖点，从差评中提炼差异化卖点）。

4. 先对产品卖点进行粗略提炼，再进行扩充和润色。

5. 检查已经完成的产品卖点是否通俗易懂、整齐美观、语句通顺、拼写正确。

Example（案例分析）

下文演示了总结产品卖点（Bullet Points）的简易操作。我们随意选取一种亚马逊平台在售产品，比如这款乐高创意拼装玩具盒（图1-8）。

图1-8 乐高创意拼装玩具盒

首先，进行Customer questions & answers 顾客问答（图1-9）的归纳，发现位居前三位的常见问题是"How many pieces?"（有多少片积木？）、"How heavy the box?"（玩具盒有多重？）、"Can you actually build a car（most important） and the other stuff shown in the pic with this set?”（用玩具盒里的插片是不是真的能拼装出一辆汽车和图画中其他的东西?）。所以这三个问题的答案就是我们在撰写产品要点时需要包含进去的内容。

Customer questions & answers
Have a question? Search for answers

Question: How many pieces?
Answer: It has 221 pieces Jean. My daughter 10 just loves it, creating whatever she can imagine.
By James Ventress on August 1, 2015
See more answers (3)
10 votes

Question: how heavy the box?
Answer: The box itself is just cardboard and the lid is a thick plastic. It's pretty light.
By Lori Wrenn on June 24, 2015
See more answers (5)
6 votes

Question: Can you actually build a car (most important!) and the other stuff shown in the pic with this set? Thanks!
Answer: Yes! My daughter made several of the objects at the same time. There were enough of each piece needed
By Mar92 on March 26, 2015
See more answers (1)
4 votes

Question: If I already have a few other lego sets would they be likely to fit into the box with these legos?
Answer: If you have a lot then prob not all of them..but if you have like 200 pieces I'm plenty sure they will fit
By Probie05 on July 27, 2015
2 votes

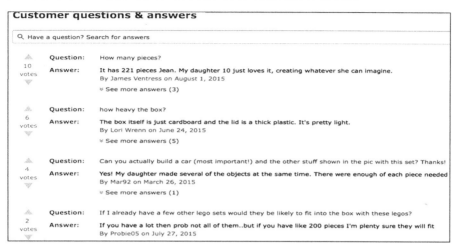

图 1 – 9　乐高创意拼装玩具盒顾客问答

其次，进行 Customer reviews 顾客评价归纳（图 1 – 10）。可大致归纳出买家关心的商品的卖点，把这些买家反馈较多的点整理起来，即可作为体现产品卖点的一个重要参考数据。图 1 – 10 中，“产品品牌”“插片数目”“产品包装”“产品用途”等都是客户关注度较高的方面，在撰写产品卖点时也要尽量包含进去。

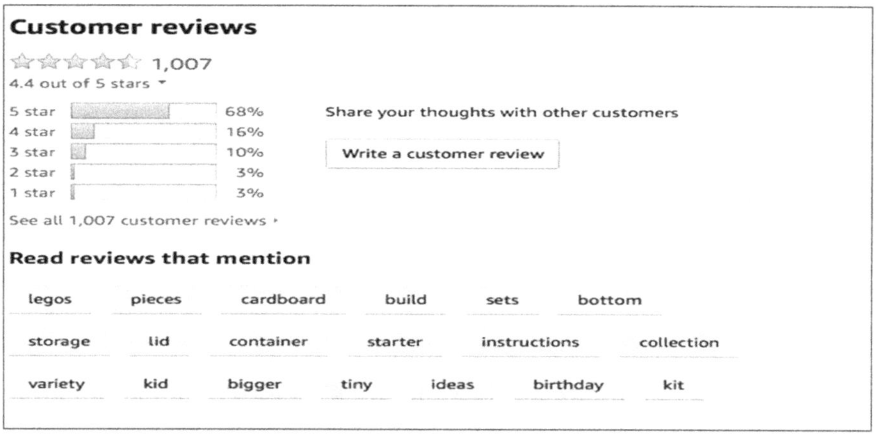

图 1 – 10　乐高创意拼装玩具盒顾客评价

我们找到了消费者关注的焦点之后，就需要根据产品基本信息，将消费者关注的焦点信息提取并列举出来。消费者关注信息提取如下：

品牌（Brand）：乐高（LEGO）；

产品名称（Product）：创意拼装玩具盒（Creative Brick Box）；

插片数量（Pieces）：484 片（484 pcs）；

尺寸（Size）：一个纸箱（One Pack；One Cardboard）；

功能（Function）：拼装汽车等形状（Build your own vehicles and much more）。

如果感觉焦点内容较少，素材不够，可以加入一些消费者未提到的，但是相对比较重要的内容。在我们的乐高玩具案例中,对于玩具,一个重要但被消费者忽视的点就是颜色,玩具颜色太单一可能不会引起消费者的购买欲望。另一个重要但被忽视的点就是玩具盒内的插片种类。只有一种形状的插片是不可能拼装出汽车或者房子的。那么补充内容如下:

颜色(Colors):35 种不同颜色(35 different colors);

插片种类(Containers):窗户、眼睛、车胎、车轮轴和其他插片(Windows, eyes, tires, wheel rims and more bricks)。

最后一步,将焦点内容和补充内容都准备好,我们就可以进行信息拼接、润色和语言结构的调整。

产品名称:创意拼装玩具盒→经典的创意拼装玩具盒:Classic Creative Brick Box;

功　　能:拼装汽车等形状→使用有 35 种不同颜色的经典乐高插片拼装属于自己的汽车等形状:Build your own vehicles and much more with this classic collection of LEGO bricks in 35 different colors;

插片数量:484 片插片→无论男女老幼都能拼装的 484 片插片:484 pieces—For boys and girls between the age of 4 and 99 years old。

经过语言润色、信息组合和语言结构调整,最终的产品卖点将会以图 1-11 所示的形式呈献给消费者。

图 1-11　乐高创意拼装玩具盒产品卖点

Practice(练习):**Find out and conclude bullet points**(找出并总结产品要点).

Activity 4　Product description(产品描述).

首先厘清产品描述的作用、原则及与产品卖点的关系。产品描述可以被看作对产品要点的补充和延伸,用来丰富产品信息内容,使消费者能够全面了解产品。一般情况下,产品描述长度不超过 2 000 个字符,必须做到"突出产品,用户至上,真实可靠,简洁易懂,拒绝抄袭"。

一份合格的产品描述一般包括基本描述(Brief Description)和详细描述(Detailed Description)两部分。基本描述多使用简单易懂的词句,主要作用在于将该产品与其他产品区别开来。详细描述一般使用较大段的文字,主要作用在于将该产品的特性、功能、服务、包装及运输等内容向买家做详细说明。详细描述的主要内容大致包括:

1. 针对品牌或者生产企业的介绍。

2. 产品的使用指标、参数、功能、特性、优势等具体信息。
3. 产品的包装及有关附属零件的说明。
4. 产品的质量认证、环保标识等信息。
5. 产品的付款方式及运输方式。
6. 产品的售后服务和质保延保等服务。
7. 多方位、多角度的产品图片。

继续以亚马逊平台为例来讲解产品描述的撰写。产品描述一般位于提问项目（Have a question？）下方，有时叫作产品描述（Product Description），有时叫作产品信息（Product Information），有时叫作产品特性（Product Specification）（图1-12）。

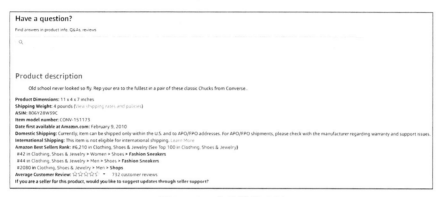

图1-12　产品描述示例

Notes（解析）

如何撰写产品描述？

1. 总结产品信息，作出基本描述。
2. 在产品卖点（Bullet Points）基础上补充内容作出详细描述，可用陈述句、疑问句形式；在撰写基本描述和详细描述时，应当遵循"FAB原则"，即：Feature（属性）+ Affect（作用）+ Benefit（利益）原则。
3. 上传产品照片。
4. 对初步完成的产品描述进行语言和格式上的优化。
5. 反复检查，产品描述中一定不能出现下列内容：
   （1）卖家姓名及具体联系方式。
   （2）网站网址。
   （3）店铺内售卖的其他产品的信息。
   （4）虚假宣传。
   （5）未经官方授权使用的品牌商标。
   （6）被严格限制和禁止使用的内容。

Example（案例分析）

在亚马逊平台上任意选取一件防水蓝牙耳机（图1-13）。

第一步，总结提炼出五个产品卖点：HD Sound（高清声音）；Magnetic（磁性耳机不易掉）；Sweat Proof（防水防汗）；Secure Fit（佩戴安全）；Lifetime Sweat Proof Warranty（终身包换）。针对这五个卖点进行补充和扩展作为该产品的详细产品描述。

图1-13　亚马逊主站蓝牙耳机产品

• HD Sound：These buds feature 8mm speakers that deliver HD audio fine-tuned for a listening experience so crisp and clear you'll swear you're listening live. And you'll be able to play it loud, as your ear-buds have been specially designed to pump out more bass and more volume without distortion.

• Magnetic：The only people that weren't surprised were our audio engineers, who determined that the patented Comply T-400 memory-foam ear tips were the perfect complement to their design, and insisted that we include them in the final product. They even threatened to hack the coffee machine if we didn't listen. Based on the awesome feedback we've gotten from customers——we're glad we did！

• Sweat Proof：Any athlete (or anyone who's worn their buds on a hot summer's day) knows that a single, well-placed drop of sweat can ruin an otherwise good headset. We've got you covered there too. Each Phaiser headset comes with a water resistant Na-no coating courtesy of our friends at Liquipel.

• Secure Fit：Our test groups were blown away by the sound quality our engineers were able to produce, but what they didn't expect was that ear-buds with such high quality audio would be so comfortable to wear.

• Lifetime Sweat Proof Warranty：1 Year Warranty / 30 Day Hassle-Free Returns.

第二步，耳机是"Phaiser"品牌的，可以对品牌进行介绍作为产品的基本描述。

From PHAISER, the Choice of 400 Thousand + Music LoversHey there！

Imagine a wireless headset that sounds even better than wired…

One that wouldn't slip out during workouts (or while sweating under the hot summer sun)…

Or hurt after hours of listening to your favorite tracks (with the volume at 11)…

Imagine a wireless headset that knew you so well, it would give you the perfect, comfortable fit every time you put it on…

And hit you with the just right amount of bass to power your next run or workout…

第三步，基本描述和详细描述完成之后，需要选取一些图片展示产品（图1-14）。对图片有三点要求是必须做到的：

（1）图片必须清晰，像素不能低于百万。

(2)产品在图片中至少要占到80%的面积。

(3)图片背景必须干净整齐,不能杂乱。

图1-14 蓝牙耳机产品描述

第四步,我们在 Word 文档中找到"工具栏",在里面选择"拼写检查",检查基本描述和详细描述中单词的拼写是否正确。

第五步,确认单词无误、照片清晰后,再做最后的上传工作,效果如图1-15所示。

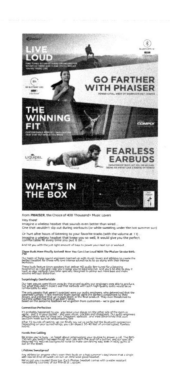

图1-15 蓝牙耳机产品完整描述展示

Practice(练习):Choose a product, write down a brief description and a detailed description(任选产品并完成其基本描述和详细描述).

Task 3　Increasing Your Exposure Rate 提升产品曝光率

学会了制作美观的产品详情页之后,下一个任务就是吸引更多的消费者观看它。这涉及一个简单的概念"曝光率"。在电子商务领域中,曝光率一般指在一定时间内某件产品或者某家店铺信息在购物平台上被买家看到的次数。曝光率的高低决定着产品被展示的次数,产品被展示次数越多,被买家点击浏览并购买的可能性才越大。因此,如何提升曝光率也成为重中之重。亚马逊平台与曝光率相关的主要有三个因素:流量(Traffic)、转化率(Conversion Rate)、排名(Rank)。

(1)流量(Traffic):通常指一个网站或网页的访问或浏览次数。时长小于1分钟的流量被称为垃圾流量;时长超过3分钟的流量才是有效流量;时长超过6分钟属于高质量流量。有效流量和高质量流量才是卖家最想获得的。

Notes(解析)

如何获得高质量的流量呢?流量分为外部流量和内部流量两种。外部流量的获得一般需要社交网站的支持和推广。例如:在Facebook和Instagram上做广告推广。内部流量的获得一般需要从两个方面着手:一个是精准地选取关键词;另一个是在购物平台做付费广告。相应地,卖家也可以利用付费广告来验证关键词选取的是否准确。

(2)转化率(Conversion Rate):指在一定时间内,所有到达卖家店铺并产生购买行为的人数和所有到达卖家店铺的人数的比率。转化率越高,说明越多的潜在消费者转变成了实际购买者。

Notes(解析)

如何提高转化率呢?精准定位关键词,使用曝光率高的关键词;突出产品特点,不要机械地排列和堆叠特点;将产品按上传时间、售卖价格和产品评价等进行细分排列;优化产品描述,特别注意使用高质量图片;对交易中遇到的问题及负面评价给予及时反馈。

(3)排名(Rank):产品排名主要由产品评价、产品评分及转化率决定。排名位居前列的产品,订单量一般会有飞跃式的增长,流量和销售量也会提升。

Notes(解析)

如何提升产品排名呢?
1. 优化产品详情页:精准的关键词、创新的长尾词及美观的图片缺一不可。
2. 产品定价要充分考虑消费者心理,价格不要太过高于平均水平。
3. 卖家对各类问题的及时反馈。
4. 卖家准备充足的库存。
5. 降低差评率和投诉率。

Cross-border E-commerce English-Chinese Vocabulary(跨境电商英汉术语对照)

产品描述常用词
材质类
1. wood	n.	木头
2. marble	n.	大理石
3. zinc	n.	锌

4. stainless steel	*n.*		不锈钢
5. glass	*n.*		玻璃
6. ceramic	*n.*		陶瓷
7. solid brass	*n.*		青铜
8. brass	*n.*		黄铜
9. copper	*n.*		红铜
10. poly/resin	*n.*		树脂
11. aluminum	*n.*		铝
12. wicker	*n.*		藤
13. steel	*n.*		钢
14. acrylic	*n.*		亚克力
15. plastic	*n.*		塑料，塑胶
16. crystal	*n.*		水晶
17. metal	*n.*		金属
18. leather	*n.*		皮
19. faux leather	*n.*		仿皮
20. wrought iron	*n.*		锻铁

颜色类

1. silver	*adj.*	银色的
2. ivory	*adj.*	象牙白的
3. amber	*adj.*	琥珀色的
4. orange	*adj.*	橘色的
5. purple	*adj.*	紫色的
6. pink	*adj.*	粉红色的
7. green	*adj.*	绿色的
8. brown	*adj.*	棕色的
9. black	*adj.*	黑色的
10. red	*adj.*	红色的
11. gold	*adj.*	金色的
12. hand-painting	*adj.*	手工彩绘的
13. gray	*adj.*	灰色的
14. dark	*adj.*	深色的
15. blue	*adj.*	蓝色的
16. white	*adj.*	白色的
17. chrome	*adj.*	铬色的
18. antique brass	*adj.*	古铜色的
19. light	*adj.*	浅色的
20. antique pewter	*adj.*	仿青灰色的
21. plating	*adj.*	电镀的

| 22. brushed steel | adj. | 沙镍色的 |
| 23. crackled | adj. | 裂纹的 |

形状类

1. square	n.	正方形
2. rectangle	n.	长方形
3. round	n.	圆形
4. oval	n.	椭圆形
5. hexagon	n.	六边形
6. octangle	n.	八边形
7. triangle	n.	三角形
8. abnormity	n.	异形
9. drum shade	n.	桶

详情页页面常见词

1. Best Sellers Rank	类目热卖排名
2. Hot New Releases	新品热卖
3. Movers and Shakers	上升最快
4. Most Wished for	添加愿望夹最多
5. Gift Ideas	适宜作为礼品
6. Any Department	任意类目
7. one-time only offer	仅此一次报价
8. bargain	折扣价
9. deal	特价
10. essential	必需品
11. multi-use	多功能
12. Review	产品评价
13. Add to Cart	加入购物车
14. Product Listing	产品详情页
15. Product Title	产品标题
16. Keywords	关键词
17. Fulfillment by Amazon（FBA）	由亚马逊完成发货配送
18. Prime	亚马逊买家会员（特权是FBA发货免运费）
19. Bullet Points	（产品）卖点
20. Product Description	产品描述
21. Traffic	流量
22. Exposure Rate	曝光率
23. Conversion Rate	转化率

Project 2

Commonplace Services（公共信息）

Learning Aims（学习目标）

From learning this chapter, students will have a good command of the following skills.
1. Be able to read and modify the terms of payment, freight and after-sale.
2. Be able to write a company profile.
3. Be able to write brand stories.
4. Learn to translate all kinds of commonplace services and master the correct English expressions.

Lead-in Situation（项目背景）

飞鱼贸易公司在速卖通平台上开立了一家户外用品专营店，客服 Judy 专门负责店内的各项公共信息建设与维护。Judy 通过浏览速卖通平台和其他主流跨境电商平台上的同类店铺，发现公共信息对于赢得客户信任、吸引客户下单、指导客户顺利完成交易有重要作用。因此推断，要想完善店铺内的各项公共信息，必须了解公共信息的类别，同时学会地道的英语表达。

Green-hand Guide（新手指南）

跨境出口电商平台的相关公共信息主要包括产品相关信息、支付相关信息、货运相关信息、售后相关信息、评价相关信息、常见问题相关信息以及店铺和品牌相关信息。不同的跨境电商平台对公共信息的要求有所不同。在交易过程中，客户希望获得的与商品交易有关的各类公共信息如下。

2 产品分组与产品信息 模块分类

一、Commonplace Information About the Product（产品相关的公共信息）

在产品相关的公共信息中，我们侧重学习产品描述、产品详情以外的相关公共信息。例如：产品使用场合、产品的搭配效果、产品选购或使用指南等。此类相关公共信息能够引导客户更好地了解产品的核心功能、准确地选购适合自己的产品，也能够指导客户使用所描述的产品，使产品发挥最大的效能。良好的产品类公共信息，能在客户浏览商品时激发客户内心的美好感觉，从而刺激客户产生强烈的购买欲望。

二、Commonplace Information About the Payment（支付相关的公共信息）

在支付相关的各类信息中，卖家一定要确保注明支付完成的时间期限、所支持的支付方式。

三、Commonplace Information About the Freight（货运相关的公共信息）

在货运相关的公共信息中必须包括客户需要支付的货运的有关费用（包括各类税费）、货物投递所需时间（包括备货时间）、货物包装、货运中不可抗力因素的描述等有关内容。

四、Commonplace Information About the After-sales Service（售后相关的公共信息）

在售后相关的公共信息中应从保障消费者权益、为客户提供周到良好的服务角度出发，写明退换货的有关细则、店铺内提供的有关售后保障内容、客户在退换货以及申请售后保障需要注意的事项等内容。

五、Commonplace Information About the Customer Reviews（客户评价相关的公共信息）

跨境电商平台十分注重客户对商家的评价，因此卖家必须说明客户的评价十分重要，并适当运用引导性语言鼓励客户给出五星好评；还要说明如果客户在收到货物后发现有任何疑问，一定要及时联系客服解决，客服会给出满意答复。

六、About the Commonplace Problems（有关常见问题）

因为客户在购买商品时会有一些基本常见问题，所以根据邮件中提问较多的内容，整理出一份常见问题及答案，会便于客户在选购时快速获得有关信息。

七、Commonplace Information About the Enterprise（the Store）[企业（店铺）相关的公共信息]

这一部分公共信息主要包括企业简介、品牌理念、团队成员、会员制度与福利等方面的内容。下面，针对这七种公共信息分别予以案例解析。

一、Commonplace Information About the Product（产品相关的公共信息）

（一）产品使用（适用）信息

以敦煌网某家户外用品专卖店为例，在滑雪裤的销售页面，商家除提供了详细的产品描述外，还附加了此商品的适用户外场景，如登山、滑雪等，并在相应场景中再次强调了产品的核心性能，如图2-1所示。

图2-1 敦煌网户外滑雪裤适用场景

（二）产品选购信息

对于服饰，选购正确的尺码是每一个客户关心的问题，在此家户外用品专卖店的服饰尺寸选购方面，有相关的测量指南，这将帮助客户更为准确地获取适合自己的服装尺码，如图2-2、图2-3所示。

图2-2　服饰尺码选购信息

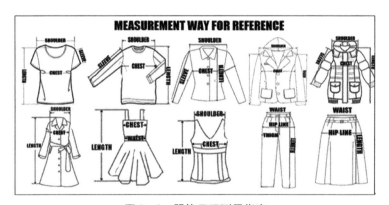

图2-3　服饰尺码测量指南

（三）产品搭配信息

在亚马逊平台上，在Levis李维斯品牌牛仔裤的产品页面，商家提供了与牛仔裤配套的服饰，不仅增强了牛仔裤的穿着效果，也给李维斯的其他商品进行了宣传推广，如图2-4所示。

图2-4　牛仔裤搭配信息

二、Commonplace Information About the Payment（支付相关的公共信息）

因为客户打算下单购买时要进入支付环节，所以商家应说明购买流程以及支持的各种支付方式。建议以图文加文字的形式给客户提供引导和帮助，如图 2-5 所示。

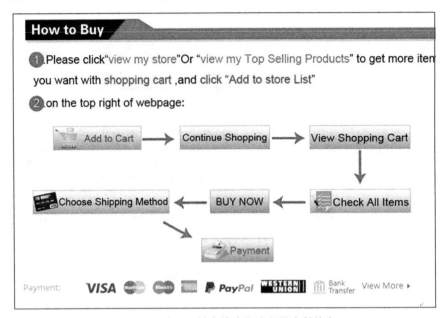

图 2-5　敦煌网某店铺购物流程及支付信息

三、Commonplace Information About the Freight（货运相关的公共信息）

在货运相关的公共信息中，应特别说明客户应当承担的税费以及到货的时间，并对货物运输中诸如天气等不可抗力因素导致的货物迟滞做出说明。在货运相关的公共信息中，敦煌网、速卖通、亚马逊三大平台之间有所区别，如图 2-6～图 2-9 所示。

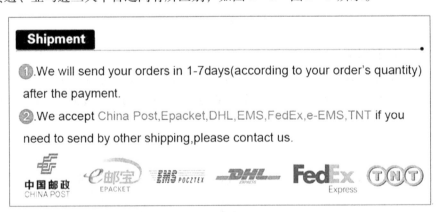

图 2-6　敦煌网某店铺发运信息

Logisitics company	Estimate Delivery Time
China Post air mail free shipping	15-60 business days
ePacktet	5-20 business days
EMS	5-15 business days
DHL	3-10 business days
FedEx	3-10 business days
TNT	3-10 business days

③.The delivery time is only for your reference

图 2–7　速卖通某店铺发运信息

Calculate your shipping cost by country/region and quantity.
Quantity: 1　Ship to: United States

Shipping Company	Shipping Cost	Estimated Delivery Time	Tracking Information
ePacket	US $8.37 Free Shipping	12-20 days	Available
AliExpress Standard Shipping	US $9.04 US $3.62 You save: US $5.42 (about 60%)	19-39 days	Available
AliExpress Premium Shipping	US $12.62	10-15 days	Available
EMS	US $40.17 US $20.08 You save: US $20.09 (about 50%)	12-21 days	Available
Fedex IE	US $47.67 US $21.45 You save: US $26.22 (about 55%)	8-16 days	Available
DHL	US $57.54 US $25.89 You save: US $31.65 (about 55%)	6-13 days	Available
UPS Express Saver	US $57.93 US $26.06 You save: US $31.87 (about 55%)	5-8 days	Available
Fedex IP	US $59.91 US $26.96 You save: US $32.95 (about 55%)	5-8 days	Available

图 2–8　亚马逊平台商品发运信息

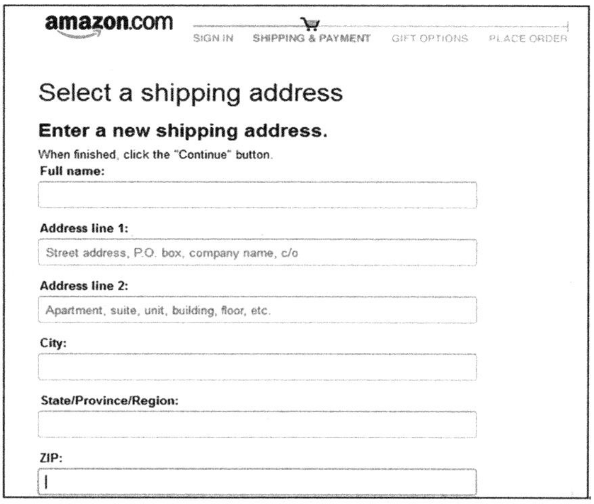

amazon.com

SIGN IN　SHIPPING & PAYMENT　GIFT OPTIONS　PLACE ORDER

Select a shipping address

Enter a new shipping address.
When finished, click the "Continue" button.
Full name:

Address line 1:
Street address, P.O. box, company name, c/o

Address line 2:
Apartment, suite, unit, building, floor, etc.

City:

State/Province/Region:

ZIP:

图 2–9　亚马逊发货地址信息

四、Commonplace Information About the After-sales Service（售后相关的公共信息）

在售后相关的公共信息中，不同的跨境电商平台有不同的展现形式，一般商家会就退换条款、保修条款进行说明，为客户提供无忧的购物保障（图2-10）。

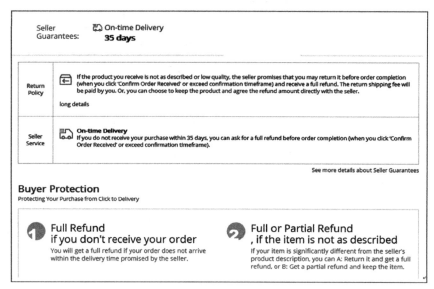

图2-10 售后公共信息

五、Commonplace Information About the Customer Reviews（客户评价相关的公共信息）

客户评价对店铺十分重要，跨境平台的商户一般都会在店铺页面强调客户好评的重要性，并强调万一客户对收到的货品存在疑问，不要贸然给店铺差评，一定要及时联系客服，客服会及时给予满意的答复，如图2-11所示。

图2-11 敦煌网某店铺客户评价的公共信息

六、About the Commonplace Problems（有关常见问题）

以服装举例，客户的常见问题会集中在服装面料特点、尺码是否标准、物流问题等方面。对于跨境电商客服人员来讲，应当注意总结客户在购买前的咨询以及客户使用产品后给出的评价与描述，及时总结客户在购买和使用当中出现的问题，如图2-12和图2-13所示。

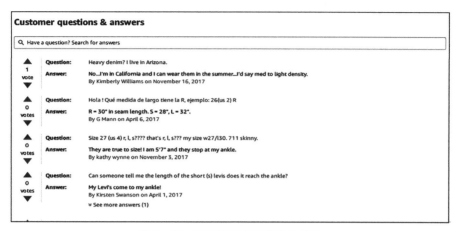

图 2-12 亚马逊客户问答公共信息

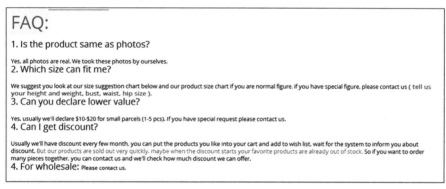

图 2-13 速卖通某女装店铺常见问题回复

Notes（解析）

（1）速卖通平台针对国际中小批发采购商与终端消费者两大类"目标客户"。就发货流程来看，速卖通卖家可以向采购商提供 Wholesale 与 Drop Shipping 两种物流服务。Wholesale 指的是采购商直接接收全部货物，在自己的仓库存货、分销；Drop Shipping 则是从速卖通卖家直接发到终端消费者，也叫直发或直运。直发需要向终端消费者收取物流费，存在收款风险。

（2）Purchase Protection Time 指速卖通平台为买家提供的收货保障期。买家若在约定期内未收到货或者货物意外损坏、被盗、丢失等，就可以要求拒付。平台会介入处理。

七、Commonplace Information About the Enterprise（the Store）[企业（店铺）相关的公共信息]

企业（店铺）相关的公共信息能够让客户更多了解即将购买的商品内涵与外延，能够拉近客户和商家的距离。一般企业简介包括公司概况、经营产品、公司特色与经营理念，体现与客户的"对话性"。品牌是店铺发展到一定阶段后逐渐成熟稳定的标志，需要一定的时间进行持续建设。图2-14所示仅为店铺的一些基本信息资料，显然还未形成自身的品牌效应，因此没有品牌故事的呈现。

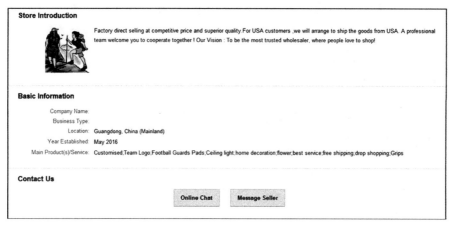

图 2-14　敦煌网某店铺信息

下面针对常用公共信息进行语言示例。

一、Normal Sentences for Shop Introduction（店铺简介常用语句）

1）公司概况常用句型：

This company was founded/established in 2000.

We have been in business since 1997/for over 20 years.

2）经营产品介绍常用句型：

We are dealing in electronic toys.

We specialize in stylish women's garments.

Our company is pioneering in the field of electronics.

Our company is among the leading manufacturers and suppliers in the field.

3）工艺特色介绍常用表达：

This company is featured with delicate embroidery and innovative designs.

We are dedicated to manufacturing high-quality goods with reasonable prices.

二、Normal Sentences for Brand Story（品牌故事常用语句）

1）公司成长历程：

The past 3 years witnessed the growth of a leading garment brand×××，who boasts superior raw materials，flexible marketing and fabulous service.

×××was proud to open its first store on AliExpress in 2013 and since then has become the front runner in the area of female fashion apparel.

2）产品定位（品质、价格、售后）：

As a growing brand，it prides itself on providing the latest and greatest fashion clothing to customers on a global scale.

As a lifestyle brand，it aims to provide trendy designs with affordable prices to young women along with providing outstanding quality and superb customer services.

3）公司经营理念：

We constantly pursue the newest trends, styles and looks you see on the catwalks and social media.

We do believe ×× × does more than adding a splash of color in clothing. It also contributes to the feels both of yours and others' in the globe.

We aim to win satisfaction, comfort and loyalty from you.

4）公司顾客观：

We aim to make sure you feel as if the world is your own personal catwalk.

×× × is simple but not commonplace. It is served for the special YOU!

Mission Implementation（任务实施）

学习了公共信息有关的知识后，Judy 也参看了一些其他企业的有关公共信息内容，接下来 Judy 开始认真准备本企业的各项公共信息内容。

Task 1　Improving Service Terms（完善服务条款）

Activity 1　Match the words according to the customer purchase process（根据客户购买流程匹配对应词语）.

1）添加到购物车。

2）继续购物。

3）浏览购物车。

4）核对全部商品。

5）立即购买。

6）选择运输方式。

7）支付。

A. Check All Items.

B. Continue Shopping.

C. Add to Cart.

D. View Shopping Cart.

E. Choose shopping method.

F. Buy Now.

G. Payment.

飞鱼公司经营多种户外用品，并且以户外服装为主，因此在产品服务相关信息中，Judy 认为最重要的是帮助客户正确选购适合自己尺码的服装，于是，她决定除了上传服装尺码对照表外，还应写出正确测量提示。

请按照中文提示内容匹配正确的英文表达方式。

Activity 2　Matching the correct English expressions according to the Chinese prompts（请按照中文提示内容匹配正确的英文表达方式）.

提示：

1）手机客户端可能无法看清尺码对照表，请收藏商品后到电脑客户端查看。

2）由于手工测量存在 1~2 厘米误差。

3）由于显示器不同色彩可能存在色差。

4）感谢您的理解！

A. Color may be a little different due to monitor!

B. Thanks for your understanding!

C. Sizes may be 2 cm – 1 inch inaccurate due to hand measure.

D. If the mobile phone client can't check the size clearly, please collect it firstly and transfer it to PC client. It would be much better.

Judy 撰写了支付政策的相关说明。

Activity 3　Fill in the blanks（填空）.

When you place _____, please make sure that _____ must be made within 3 days, otherwise your order will be _____. There are _____ for you to pay, like your credit cards, West Union and so on as requested in our list of payment terms.

A. an order

B. payment

C. cancel

D. many ways

Judy 根据速卖通网站提供的货运平台模板填写了相关信息。为更好地让客户理解相关货运政策，她对几个关键词语进行了解释。

Activity 4　Matching the correct freight forwarder according to the explanation by Judy（请根据 Judy 的解释匹配相应的货运条款）.

1) The estimated delivery date is based on the seller's handling time, the shipping service selected, and the tone when the seller receives cleared payment. In certain cases, the estimated delivery date will vary. By knowing the estimated delivery date, you can determine how long it will take to receive your item.

2) Sellers are required to specify how long they will take to package and ship the item after receiving cleared payment. Sellers may select a handling time between the same business day and the later 30 business days.

3) Some shipping services provide an estimate for the number of days that it will take the carrier to deliver the item to the buyer. This transit time does not include the seller's handling time. Transit time includes normal weekdays. Often Saturdays, Sundays, and major holidays are not included in transit time estimates.

4) A payment is considered "cleared" after your payment has been deposited into the seller's account. If you pay by using Alipay, the payment may clear immediately. However, if you pay by check, money order, your payment may take several days to clear.

5) Note: Shipping costs shown include fuel surcharges. Import duties, taxes and other customs related charges are not included. Buyers bear all responsibilities for all extra charges incurred (if any).

6) UPS shipping cost savings displayed above reflect discounts offered to AliExpress sellers. They may also include other promotions, subsidies or discounts offered by individual sellers to their buyers, and are only valid on transactions completed via AliExpress.

请根据 Judy 的解释匹配相应的货运条款。

A. About estimated delivery date.

B. About Shipping cost.

C. About cleared payment.

D. About handling time.

E. About shipping services.

F. About UPS shipping cost savings.

Judy 考虑到难免有客户对收到的货品不满或其他需要退换的情形，因此她撰写了详细的退换货政策。请根据括号内的中文内容找到相对应的英文翻译。重要信息可以通过大写或颜色变幻提示客户。

Activity 5　Matching the correct English translation according to the Chinese prompts in brackets（请根据括号内的中文内容找到相对应的英文翻译）.

（1）Return & Refund.

1）We stand behind every product we sell.（如果您对货物不满，我们接受退货）

2）As the return policy says, we need the original receipt or a record of the purchase in our system, and（产品及所有配件请原装寄回）

3）CUSTOMERS WILL BE RESPONSIBLE FOR RETURN SHIPMENT FREE.

4）It may take up to 6 business days to process your return after we receive your product.（我们会将货款退回您的支付宝）

5）（如果产品与描述不符我们将承担所有运费。）

（2）Guarantee.

6）12 months Manufacturer's limited Warranty for defective items（excluding items damaged and/or misused after receipt）.（配件享受三个月保修）

7）（问题产品需要在保修期内及时登记并寄回）（and in the original packaging, if possible）.

8）You must tell us what the defect is and give us your order number.（保修期外商品店铺不负责维修或换新）

9）You agree to all of the above-listed policies upon ordering on AliExpress.

　　A. We will refund all the money to your Alipay.

　　B. We will bear all the shipping cost if the product（s）is（are）not as advertised.

　　C. If you're not pleased with your purchase, we accept return.

　　D. THE PRODUCT MUST BE IN ITS ORIGINAL CONDITION, AND ALL THE ACCESSORIES.

　　E. WE DO NOT REPAIR OR REPLACE THE ITEMS WITH AN EXPIRED WARRANTY.

　　F. Accessories come with a 3-month warranty.

　　G. Defective items MUST BE reported and returned within the warranty period.

通过学习，Judy 十分明确客户评价的重要性，因此她针对评价也撰写了相关信息。

Activity 6　Matching the correct Chinese terms according to the relevant contents（请根据相关的内容，匹配正确的中文条款）.

A. Please take a minute to leave us a positive feedback with an overall Detailed Selling Rating (DSR) of 5, which means a lot in our future AliExpress undertakings. Your recognition is our motivation in developing our business to serve you even better.

B. If you plan to give us a neutral/negative feedback, please write to us immediately so that we can do our best to resolve your problem. A neutral/negative feedback doesn't solve any problem. Please contact us first. Thanks for your understanding on this matter.

C. If you have any question, please feel free to contact us anytime. We will do our best so that you're satisfied!

1. 表明收到货物后随时可以和客服取得联系，客服将竭诚为客户提供满意的解决方案。
2. 使客户明确五星好评对企业的重要性。
3. 建议客户一旦有任何问题，想要对店铺进行中差评，就马上联系客服，客服将帮助客户更好解决问题，恳请客户理解支持。

Task 2　Listing Some Frequently Asked Questions（常见问题列举）

Judy 从近期收到的邮件中发现了客户经常询问的一些问题，她决定将这些问题整理出来，帮助客户提高效率。

Activity 1　Find the right answers to frequently asked questions（请根据常见问题找到正确的回答）.

Q1：How do I know what size to get?

Q2：How about materials of your products? Are these made from environment-friendly materials?

Q3：How can I track my parcel?

Q4：Is there any customs tax?

Q5：What can I do when purchase protection time is running out?

Q6：Do you support wholesale?

A1：You can track your parcel on the following website using your tracking number: www.17track.net/en (Copied to the browser to open).

A2：Usually we will declare the minimum value to avoid customs tax. But due to different policies in different countries, there might be customs tax that should be paid by the buyer. So you could leave a message when placing the order about how much value you would like to declare.

A3：You can use the size chart and pay attention to the page tips.

A4：If your purchase protection time is running out, please contact us and we can help you to extend it. So your money will not go to my account.

A5：Wholesale and drop shipping are both welcomed. For wholesale, we will offer discount or free express shipping which only takes 3-7 days to arrive. For drop shipping, we could send the goods to your customers directly and won't leave information about us if you'd like to.

A6：Our products all use natural and environmental materials that are in line with international standards.

Task 3 Writing Store Descriptions（撰写店铺简介）

Activity 1 Write an English introduction of the store according to the Chinese outline（根据中文提纲撰写店铺英文简介）.

1. 说明店铺的成立时间与经营理念。
2. 介绍店铺目前的产品销量。
3. 店铺取得成绩的经验。
4. 愿意与客户建立良好、长久的合作关系。

Since establishment on July 5th, 2014 at AliExpress, Flying Fish Ltd. has built a strong team who is committed to providing the most competitive products and excellent services to global buyers. Flying Fish's sales volume tops first on AliExpress for recent years. Customers' satisfaction leads to a high credit of our store and makes us be awarded trophies by AliExpress since 2015. You can always trust us when doing business with us. We are looking forward to building a long-term business relation with you.

虽然近两年飞鱼外贸公司发展迅速，但是目前品牌知名度不高，主管告诉 Judy 要注重品牌建设；主管帮助 Judy 列出了品牌理念等内容，Judy 根据相关内容着手撰写品牌故事。

Activity 2 Write an English brand story according to the Chinese outline（根据中文提纲撰写英文品牌故事）.

1. 品牌 Flying Fish 的来由：飞鱼寓意飞翔的鱼儿，意指追求自由、崇尚自然、敢于冒险。
2. 品牌 Flying Fish 的倡导理念：时尚安全、价格合理、帮助户外爱好者挑选自己的用品。
3. 品牌 Flying Fish 的目标客户：热爱户外的人们。
4. 品牌 Flying Fish 的经营信条：私人订制的户外天堂。

Flying Fish was proud to open its first store on AliExpress in 2014 and since then has become one of the front runners in the area of outdoors. Flying Fish's name conveys freedom, nature and adventure. As a growing brand, it prides itself on providing the latest and greatest fashion outdoors to customers on a global scale.

We constantly pursue the newest trends, styles and qualities you see on the social media; only the most up-to-date developments are sourced from around the globe, combing style with quality materials to produce the outdoor goods you see in store.

Flying Fish is continuing to expand its business ensuring it remains one of AliExpress's most loved brands.

Flying Fish focuses on high-quality products that fuse wild style and active feelings with a combining way. For the more beautiful landscape, we bring extraordinary experience for people who love outdoors. Flying Fish—a private paradise for you!

Task 4 Public Information Maintaining（公共信息维护）

HAYOHA 是一家经营时尚女装的外贸公司，该公司成立于 1998 年，经过多年经营它的服装已形成了时尚、自然、舒适的特点，适合年龄在 18～35 岁年轻女性穿着。该公司于 2013 年在速卖通平台开设了第一家店铺，面向全球销售女装。随着跨境电商的繁荣发展，店铺管理经营也日臻完善。HAYOHA 电商中心根据最近的客户反馈，决定进一步完善店铺有关的公共信息内容。

由于近期有客户总是在支付环节超时，客服 Marry 准备补充支付条款。

Activity 1　Please translate the following terms into English（请将下列条款翻译成英文）。

1. 支持支付宝。

2. 你可以使用 VISA 等多种支付方式。

3. 付款必须在下单三天内完成。

4. 所有付款通过第三方安全管理。

Activity 2　Translate the sentences in brackets according to the background of the case（根据案例背景，翻译括号内的句子）.

HAYOHA：Target audience is the fashion conscious 18 – 35 women. (We aim to offer our customers the fashion what they want.) To stay in touch with the ever changing trends within our market, we have developed a dynamic and very responsive organization.

_____

We realize the most important part of our business is the customer. (That is why we focus on delivering an exciting shopping experience and making sure that our high standards of quality, value for money and services are always met.)

_____

_____

(Our team is a highly dedicated and motivated group of individuals.)

_____

We firmly focused on your needs. We hope that with continuous developments and renovations we will focus on bringing our unique experience to shoppers.

Cross-border E-commerce English-Chinese Vocabulary（跨境电商英汉术语对照）

1. place an order		下订单
2. payment	*n.*	支付、付款
3. shipping fee		运费
4. tax	*n.*	税
5. guarantee	*vt. & n.*	保证、确保
6. maintenance	*n.*	维护、产品维修
7. measurement	*n.*	尺寸
8. company profile		公司简介
9. brand story		品牌故事
10. be in the line of		从事于、经营
11. return or refund		退换货
12. warranty	*n.*	质保
13. duty	*n.*	关税
14. fashion	*n.*	时尚
15. environmental protection		环保

16. nature	n.	自然
17. track	n. & vt	踪迹，追踪
18. inaccuracy	n.	错误、不精确
19. outdoors	n. & adj.	户外，户外的
20. apparel	n.	服装
21. collect additional fees		征收额外费用
22. brokerage fees		中间手续费
23. delivery time		发货时间
24. customs clearing		清关
25. file a claim		要求索赔
26. ePacket	n.	国际 e 邮宝
27. chart	n.	图表
28. feature	vt.	以……为特色，主营
29. incur damage		发生破损
30. replacement	n.	更换
31. quality control		质检
32. recover the cost of damage or less		承担破损或丢件的费用
33. neutral/negative feedback		中差评

Project 3

Pre-sale Consulting（售前咨询）

Learning Aims（学习目标）

From learning this chapter, students can reply to customers' mails from the information center on Cross-border E-commerce Platform, deal with pre-sale consulting, guide consumption and promote sales effectively.

1. Understand the common customer consulting in the pre-sale phase.
2. Exercise the ability to understand the core information of the buyer's consulting.
3. To master the pre-sale communicating skills related to products' functions, logistics problems, payment methods, etc.

Lead-in Situation（项目背景）

小熊贸易公司在速卖通平台上开立了一家服装店，客服专员 Peter 和 Anne 专门负责客户的售前咨询，类似于线下零售店铺的导购人员。售前咨询在国际贸易领域称为"询盘"（enquiry），是指交易的一方准备购买或出售某种商品的人向潜在的供货人或买主探寻该商品的成交条件或交易的可能性的业务行为，它不具有法律上的约束力。但是，对于 B2C 跨境零售业务，及时确定地回复顾客咨询，是提升店铺转化率的关键指标。根据速卖通平台大数据分析，北美地区流量高峰在 10:00—13:00（北京时间 1:00—4:00），流量低峰在 15:00—23:00（北京时间 6:00—19:00），如果流量高峰时段的站内信或在线咨询得不到及时回复，则极有可能造成订单流失。所以，上夜班对于客服人员是件很正常的事，Peter 和 Anne 都做好了心理准备。

Green-hand Guide（新手指南）

一、Cross-border E-commerce Platform Rules（跨境电商平台规则）

为了凸显商品质量及服务能力好的卖家，提升买家购物体验，速卖通平台推出了"卖家服务等级"，考核卖家在买家服务方面的各项能力，旨在激励卖家提升店铺服务水平。

卖家服务等级每月评定一次，并于次月 3 日前在后台更新，用以考核过去 90 天卖家的经营能力，包括卖家责任裁决率和好评率，特别是买家不良体验订单率（Order Defect Rate，ODR），即买家不良体验订单占所有考核订单的比例。根据考核结果，将卖家分为优秀、良好、及格和不及格四个等级（表 3-1），不同等级的卖家将会获得不同的平台资源（表3-2）。

表3-1 卖家的四个等级

评定等级	优秀	良好	及格	不及格
评定标准	1. 考核期内结束的已支付订单数≥90笔； 2. ODR<2.5%； 3. 买家责任裁决率<0.8%； 4. 90天好评率≥97%	1. ODR<4%； 2. 买家责任裁决率<0.8%	1. 4%≤ODR<8%； 2. 买家责任裁决率<0.8%	1. ODR≥8%； 2. 买家责任裁决率≥0.8%

表3-2 不同等级卖家获得的平台资源

奖励资源	优秀	良好	及格	不及格
橱窗推荐数/个	10	5	2	0
搜索排序曝光	曝光优先+特殊标识	曝光优先	正常	曝光靠后
提前放款特权	有机会享受最高放款比例	无法享受最高放款比例	无法享受最高放款比例	无法享受最高放款比例
平台活动	优先参加	允许参加	允许参加	不允许参加
店铺活动	正常	正常	正常	活动时间和数量大幅减少
营销邮件数/个	500	200	100	无

Notes（解析）

"买家不良体验订单"指考核期限内（90天）满足以下任一条件的订单：

（1）买家给予中差评。

（2）DSR精确释义为卖家服务评级系统，包括商品描述的准确性、沟通质量及回应速度、物品运送时间的合理性中低分（商品描述≤3星或卖家沟通≤3星或物流服务=1星）。

（3）成交不卖。

（4）仲裁提交订单。

（5）卖家5天不回应纠纷导致纠纷结束。

值得注意的是，如果一个订单同时满足两个及以上的不良体验描述，只记一次，不会重复计算；若在考核期内，买家不良体验的订单来自两个及以下买家，则将不考核ODR；若因卖家责任裁决订单数仅为1，则将不考核其卖家责任裁决率。

二、Set Priontes（设置优先级）

进入速卖通消息中心（图3-1），可以自行设置消息标签，以提示优先处理级别，提升售前咨询客服的工作效率。建议优先级别设置如下：第一，等待买家付款的订单留言；第二，等待发货的订单留言；第三，等待买家收货的订单留言；第四，纠纷订单留言。请你思考一下这样安排站内信处理顺序，为何缘故？

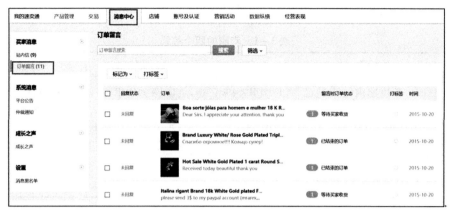

图3-1　速卖通消息中心示例

三、Common Customer Problems（常见客户问题）

（一）无法完成下单

比如客户来到亚马逊的购买页面（图3-2），但是无法完成单击"Add to Cart"按钮操作。部分客户用手机客户端登录选购产品，所以有些提示看不见，这个时候就应该想到是否是因为这个原因无法完成下单（图3-3）。

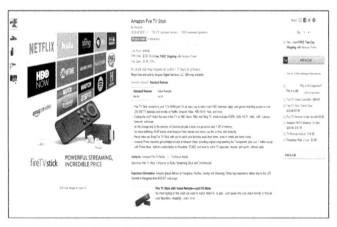

图3-2　亚马逊购买页面示例

图3-3　亚马逊购买提示示例

（二）没有需要的尺寸或颜色，无法下单

客户问题："I want light color, but there is no option there, what should I do?"对于客户提出的一些特殊的小要求，例如更改尺寸、颜色，可以告诉他们利用"Message box to seller"功能。客户选择完产品之后，请买家注明特殊需求。

客服回复："Friend, you can go ahead to place your order and leave the message in the box like: I want one more of…, then I will adjust the price for you. After I change the price, you can make payment."

大部分人会认为这时买家应该已经明白该如何操作了，实际上还是会有买家再说："Sorry, I am confused what I should do."

这个时候进一步解释说明:"Place the order but stop at the payment page. After you see the price changed to the price I told you, put your bank information on the payment page."

这样说明过后,买家就会知道如何操作了,他们也不会对修改价格有任何疑问了。这里需要提醒的是,在修改价格之前,一定要和买家沟通好;否则,买家如果不理解卖家的行为,则会去投诉卖家,卖家就有提价销售的嫌疑了。

(三)付款问题

(1)速卖通的付款方式。

目前平台支持买家通过信用卡(分人民币通道和美元通道)、Web-money、T/T 汇款、西联汇款、Qiwi Wallet、巴西 Boleto 这几种方式付款(图3-4)。

(2)买家付款不成功该如何解决。

首先询问付款不成功的原因。常见的情况有 Business Card 支付。商务卡目前在速卖通是无法支付成功的,所以建议买家换卡;买家信用卡未开通 3D 密码,所以建议买家联系发卡行开通 3D 密码。偶尔碰到发卡行不支持这种 3D 密码服务或者没听说过 3D 密码的,则直接建议更换支付方式。图3-5 所示为买家使用西联支付的页面。

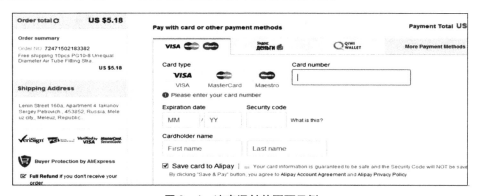

图3-4 速卖通付款页面示例

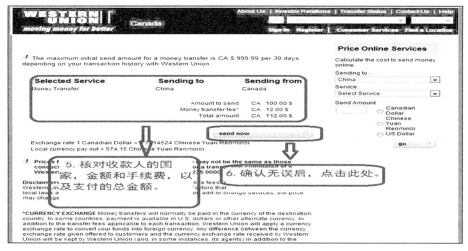

图3-5 西联支付页面示例

(3) 线下交易需谨慎。

在上述问题解决之后，如果还是不能成功付款，有些买家可能会要求使用 PayPal 这样的线下交易（图 3-6），因为它的使用人群广且快捷。这时需要谨慎处理，因为 PayPal 更多地倾向于买家的利益，所以在不得已的情况下，尽量不要使用。若要使用请注意：不可使用除 PayPal 登记注册外的地址进行发货；不可使用 Money Requested；要使用 Invoice 方式收款；不可与未注册的账户交易。

图 3-6　PayPal 交易页面

（四）为什么订单会关闭

为了保证交易的安全性，保障卖家的利益，降低后期因为盗卡等原因引起的买家拒付风险，平台会在 24 小时内对每一笔买家支付的订单（信用卡支付的）进行风险审核。如果监测到买家的资金来源有风险（如存在盗卡支付等风险），支付信息将无法通过审核，订单会被关闭。

即使订单资金审核不通过，也不会影响卖家的账户。订单关闭后，无法重新开启，平台会通知买家申诉。如果买家提供的证明（图 3-7）审核通过，则可以让买家重新下单付款。

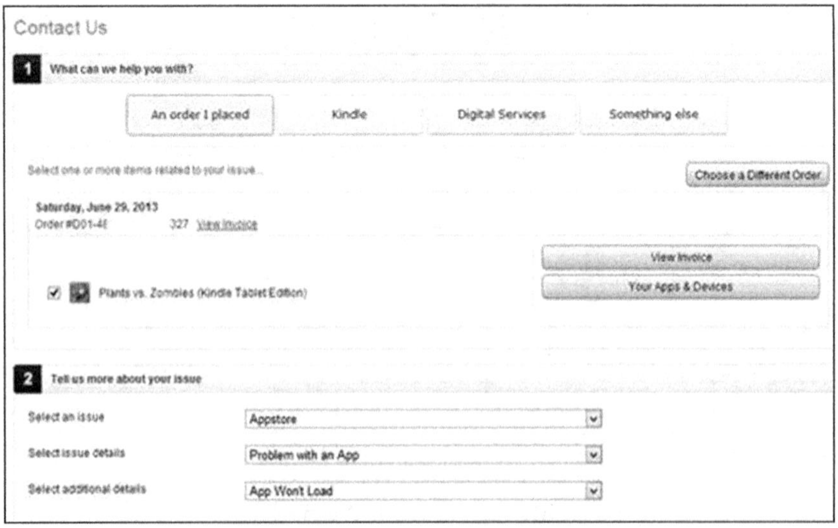

图 3-7　订单关闭后买家提交证明页面

Mission Implementation（任务实施）

了解了上述的常见问题之后，Peter 和 Anne 开始着手自己的工作，即登录跨境平台店铺后台消息中心，处理站内客户来信。

Task 1　Payment Fail Reason（支付失败的原因）

Anne 收到的客户来信表示无法完成支付，Anne 耐心地解释了可能造成支付失败的原因，请你一一甄别。

Q：Why did my payment fail?

A：If your payment for an order has failed, please check if it is due to the following situations:

- Card security code failed.

Please note that an incorrect card security code could cause payment failure. Card security code is the short numeric code on the back of your credit card. Please verify that you have entered the correct card security code and try again.

- Insufficient fund.

If you meet the insufficient fund error log when you make payment by credit card, please make sure that you have sufficient fund in your account and that payment for your order does not exceed your credit limit.

Please also make sure you have used a Visa or MasterCard personal credit card to finish payment, because at present debit card or business card is unable to be supported.

- The credit card type accept ed and not accepted.

When you choose Visa and MasterCard as payment methods, please make sure your Visa or MasterCard is a personal credit card. The following types of credit cards are currently unable to be accepted: charge cards, business/commercial cards, Visa and MasterCard debit card.

- Exceed limit.

Please make sure the order amount does not exceed your credit card limit, or the payment is unable to go through smoothly.

- The 3-D security code failed.

Please make sure that:

(1) Your credit card has been authorized by your credit card issuer to make an online payment by activating 3-D security code.

(2) Your credit card has activated 3-D security code. If you have not activated 3-D security code, please contact your card issuer with this issue.

(3) The 3-D security code for Visa is called Verified by Visa (VBV) and for Master Card is called MasterCard Secure Code.

Task 2　Replying to Enquiry for Unspecified Products（回复不确定产品的询盘）

Peter 收到询盘，但客户没有说明需要哪种产品，Peter 回复要求客户提供产品链接。请阅读英文信件内容找出与想要表达的汉语意思的匹配句。

Q：How much for it, if the foot length 26cm, width 8cm?

A:

> Hello, Glad to receive your enquiry. According to your enquiry I do not know which style you need because we have so many types shown on the websites. Please let me know the detailed model according to our websites. Would you please provide the links for the products you are interested in?
>
> You are welcome to add our Skype ××× or MSN ××× for further discussion. We are expecting to establish a long-term business relation with you. We are Looking forward to hearing from you soon.
>
> Regards
>
> Peter

（1）对他的询盘表示感谢。

（2）要求客户提供他感兴趣产品的链接。

（3）有需要的话把我们的 Skype 和 MSN 给客户。

Notes（解析）

对于客户询问鞋子尺码的问题，由于国外的鞋子尺码和国内的标准是不一样的，而且有些国家客户的脚长等测量标准是英寸的，而中国使用厘米，因此店铺在销售这些对于尺码有要求的产品时，在发布产品的详情页里要设置好详细的尺码对照表。

Task 3　Replying to Enquiry for Product Size（回复产品尺寸询盘）

Peter 收到一位比利时客户 Alaim LIESSE 对棉夹克尺寸的询盘内容如下：

> Hi, I'd like to order the jacket, but I hesitate about the size. Here are my real actual body measurements:
>
> —chest (body measurement): 93 cm = 36.6 inch
>
> —waist (body measurement): 88 cm = 34.6 inch
>
> —hip (body measurement): 102 cm = 40.2 inch
>
> —shoulders (body measurement): 47 cm = 18.5 inch
>
> Here are complementary coat measurements:
>
> —sleeve length (jacket measurement): 62 cm = 24.4 inch
>
> —jacket length (jacket measurement): 71cm = 28 inch
>
> For your information, my total height is 178cm (70.1inch) and my weight is 65kg (152 pounds).
>
> Cam you please advise me before I place my order?
>
> Thank you very much,
>
> Alaim LIESSE

Peter 回复如下，请翻译。

Dear Alaim,

Thanks for your enquiry. I think size 2XL fits you. If you have any question, please contact us. Have a nice day!

Best wishes

Task 4　Replying to Counter Offer（回复还盘）

Activity 1　Insisting on the original price（坚持原价）.

Anne 收到客户 Svetlana 对鞋子要求折扣的邮件"May you discount the price of these shoes?"，回信告知只购买一件产品不能给他折扣，如果购买 10 件以上可以给 5% 的折扣。请按此排列出恰当的语句顺序。

Dear Svetlana,

Thanks for your enquiry.

_____

_____

Best regards, Anne

A. Looking forward to your favorable reply.

B. From the product feedback, I trust you will agree that our price is competitive for such good quality.

C. However, we can give a 5% discount for bulk purchase of no less than 10 PCs.

D. Discount can not be provided for 1pc as we only have minimum profit.

E. Thank you for your understanding.

Notes（解析）

对女性而言购物是一大乐事，但懂得如何还价，懂得如何用最少的钱买高质量的东西，才能真正体会到购物的乐趣，所以女性往往喜欢还价。在客户还价时，作为一名客服，应当根据具体情况，做出适当的反应。如果不同意客户还价，客服可向客户反复强调所有能抵消价格的因素，如产品质量、外观、效用、功能、售后服务等。

Activity 2　Making a concession（给予折扣）.

Anne 收到客户 Nn Shel 要求打折的邮件"Ask to reduce the total price"，因为这位是他们店里最受欢迎的老顾客，所以 Anne 同意给她折扣。请问，如果原价是 $8.5，Anne 同意卖给客户的最终价格是多少?

Dear Nn,

Thanks for your enquiry.

As you are our most welcomed friend, we decide to give you a 10% discount for the product. I trust you will find the price has reached the bottom in consideration of its quality.

Wish you a happy shopping with us.

Best regards,

Anne

Notes（解析）

英语中表示"打折"，讲的是减价的比例，如：a 20% discount，意思是20%折扣，即打八折，这和中国人讲的减价后实付占原价的几成是不同的。另外，打八折，英语也可说：20% off。

Task 5　Urging the Placement of an Order（敦促下单）

客户 Julia 对手提包相关信息进行询问后，接着问 Peter 是否有货。

Julia：Hello, what size is this bag? Height? Length? Thanks!

Peter：Hello, dear friend, the length of this bag is 28cm, the width is 12cm and the height is 20cm. Hope this information will help you.

Julia：Hello, yes thanks…I want to buy this bag…I want GRAY color. Thanks! Do you have a gray one in stock?

Peter 答复产品有货，并催促客户下单。排列下列句子，完成一封催单信。

Dear Julia,

Thank you for your enquiry.

_____

_____

Best regards,

Peter

A. Please place your order as soon as possible.

B. Right now, we only have 2 lots left.

C. Since it is very popular, the products have a high risk of selling out soon.

D. Yes, we have this item in stock. How many do you want?

Notes（解析）

回复客户的询盘后，要关注客户的邮件或者订单情况。如果客户下了订单，那就可以准备发货了。但是如果站内信回复2~3天后客户没有反应，那么客服人员就需要及时给客户再写一封站内信，催促下单。催单可以分两次跟进，第一次3~7天，第二次20天左右。

Task 6　Urging Payment（敦促支付）

Peter 接到客户 Polly 的新订单，但是发现客户未付款，于是写信给客户，委婉提醒其付款。将英文按照信件内容排序对号入座，整理成完整站内信。

Hello Polly,

1. 感谢下单。

2. 发现未付款。

3. 提醒完成支付。

4. 愈早支付愈早收货。

5. 有支付问题随时帮助解决。

6. 提示付款链接。

Best regards,

Peter

A. This is a friendly reminder to you to complete the payment transaction as soon as possible.

B. However, we notice that you have not made the payment yet.

C. Instant payments are very important, because the earlier you pay, the sooner you will get the item.

D. We appreciated your purchase from us.

E. If you have any problem in making the payment, or if you do not want to go through with the order, please let us know. We can help you resolve the payment problem.

F. Please check the following link: *http://help.aliexpress.com/pay order.html*. Thanks again.

Notes（解析）

客户下单后，未付款的原因可能有以下几点：

（1）客户很犹豫到底要不要买。

（2）客户觉得价格有点高。

（3）客户在选择货物时出现一些问题。

所以，在写催促客户付款的邮件时要注意以下几点：

（1）强调产品的卖点。

（2）付款后可以早日安排发货，以免缺货。

（3）不要催得太紧，以免让客户反感。

Task 7　Informing Short Supply of Goods（通知缺货）

Anne 收到客户 Vadim 对棉夹克的询盘，查看库存后发现该款棉夹克目前没货，三周后才能有货，于是写信告诉客户并向客户推荐其他替代品。请补全下面的邮件内容。

Dear Vadim,

Thanks for your enquiry.

The item you mentioned is just ___缺货___ and will ___有货___ in three weeks. Could you please check whether the following similar ones are also suitable for you?

*http://www.aliexpress.com/store/product ******.html*.

Looking forward to your early reply.

Best regards,

Anne

Notes（解析）

有时客户会拿照片询问店家是否有他照片中的商品。如果没有货，要告诉客户什么时候会有货并推荐相似产品，同时提供相应的链接以方便其点击购买。

Task 8　Confirming the Order（确认订单）

Anne 接到一笔新订单，即一位英国客户买了三个手提包，已经付款成功。于是 Anne 写信给客户确认订单并表示感谢。请将邮件中汉语翻译成合适的英文以匹配上下文内容。

Dear Susan,

Thanks for your order. The order number is XD986.

We are now making preparations for the ___发货___, and they will ___2~3个工作日发出___ by Chinese Post Air Mail. Once we get ___运单号___, we will let you know.

> Anticipating your further orders.
> Thanks and best regards,
> Anne

Notes（解析）

收到客户的新订单，卖家要完成以下几步：

（1）点击后台的新订单，查看订单的资金审核状态。在速卖通平台上，基本的订单资金在 24 小时之后都会通过审核，那时订单就会显示为"待发货订单"。

（2）检查库存。卖家应根据客户的新订单检查库存量，如果库里没有货了，卖家就要同时下国内订单补充货源或买货。

（3）写感谢信给客户。

（4）发货后发信给客户告知已经发货和物流查询的单号。

Task 9 Making Enquiry for Product Information（产品信息咨询）

以下是客户通过即时通讯软件 Skype 向 Peter 询问夹克衫的相关产品信息

> Buyer: Hi!
> Peter: Hi, welcome to my store. What can I do for you?
> Buyer: Do you have this jacket in size 16?
> Peter: Just a moment, please. Yes, we have it in stock.
> Buyer: How many colors do you have for this jacket?
> Peter: They come in 5 colors: brown, blue, white, black and green. Which color do you prefer?
> Buyer: I prefer brown. Do you have other styles?
> Peter: Sure. I will send you some links with the latest styles.
> Buyer: Yeah, they all look beautiful. What about the quality then?
> Peter: Its quality will be a surprise to you besides the new style. Many customers have great comments on it. I'm sure you will love them.
> Buyer: I do hope so. What are they made of?
> Peter: They are made of cotton.
> Buyer: OK. Thank you very much. I'll buy a brown jacket with size 16 in style 3.
> Peter: Thanks a lot and thank you for coming to my store.

Notes（解析）

询问在销售中扮演极重要的角色，客服人员不但可以通过询问客户对产品的尺寸、颜色、款式、材质等喜好来获取所需的信息并确认客户的需要，而且能主导与客户谈话的主题。询问是最重要的沟通手段之一，它能使客户因自由表达意见而产生参与感。

与询问同样重要的还有倾听，客服人员除了提问，还得用心倾听客户的描述，这既是为了真正接近客户，也是对客户最起码的尊重。了解了客户的喜好，并与之建立了很好的沟通之后销售就变得水到渠成了。

Task 10 Making Conversation on Short Supply of Goods（缺货的沟通）

客户通过 Skype 向 Anne 询问裙子相关信息，Anne 表示她想要的商品正好无货，并向她推荐其他产品。

> Buyer: Hello, are you there? I am interested in your dresses.
> Anne: Hi, at your service.
> Buyer: Do you have this dress in purple?
> Anne: What size do you need?
> Buyer: I'd like size 6.
> Anne: Size 6 in purple is out of stock at present. But we have other colors in stock: red, grey, blue and yellow. You can choose them.
> Buyer: Sorry, I like purple best.
> Anne: We'll get more in one week. Will you please try us in one week?
> Buyer: I'm very busy. I am afraid I don't have much time to visit your store then.
> Anne: Then do you like other similar styles? They look alike, but their materials are different. This one is made of cotton, and that one is made of silk, so it costs 20 dollars more. Can you accept it?
> Buyer: Can you give me the link?
> Anne: Wait a moment please.

(After a while, Anne sent a link.)

> Anne: Please click on the link and you'll see the silk dress.
> Buyer: How nice the color is. Is it made of pure silk?
> Anne: Yes, so it feels very smooth.
> Buyer: Well, I wonder if the silk piece's color won't go off.
> Anne: In fact, the colors of all the silk dresses here are guaranteed against fading.
> Buyer: Great!
> Anne: But please wash it in lukewarm soap water and rinse well. Don't rub or wring it. And please don't hang it out in the sunshine.
> Buyer: That's really very thoughtful of you. Thank you for your advice.
> Anne: It's my pleasure.

Notes（解析）

当客户所要的产品没货时，客服应尽量详细地向他们推荐其他商品，并利用自己的专业知识来帮助客户。如果客服能诚恳而富有经验地向客户推荐时尚的设计、流行的款色以及相关的洗涤、护理知识，通常可以满足客户的要求，进而达到宾主尽欢的效果。

售前咨询服务常用句示例 Useful Sentences Pool

(1) 服务常用语。

Anything I can do for you?

Would you like some help?

May I help you?

What can I do for you?

Is there anything I can help you with?

Can I be of any assistance?

At your service.

Can I recommend some to you?

Let me check it for you.

（2）感谢客户的询盘。

Thank you for your enquiry.

Thanks for your enquiry.

We are appreciative of your enquiry.

We appreciate your enquiry.

（3）讨价还价。

That's too expensive. I can't afford to buy it.

Is the price negotiable?

It costs too much.

It's not worth that much.

You're robbing me！

Is it your best price?

Can't you quote us anything cheaper?

Can you make it cheaper?

Is it your last price?

How about 10 dollars per pair?

Can you come down a little?

Can you give me a discount?

Please give me a lower price.

Isn't it possible to give us even a little more discount?

I'm afraid that it is impossible.

We never quote two prices.

The price is fixed.

To tell you the truth, it's almost at cost price.

Sorry, we have only one price.

I'm sorry, but here is no room for bargaining.

I'm afraid that there is no room to negotiate the price.

We're practically selling at cost already.

We're on clearance sale now. Prices have been up to 30% off. Do not miss the chance.

You know we're clearing out stock now. It's a real bargain.

①表示不能接受还价。

Sorry, we cannot accept the price you suggested.

Sorry, the price you asked for is not acceptable.

②告诉客户我们的价格是很有竞争力的。

Our prices are very competitive compared with those of similar products in other stores.

Considering the superior quality of the goods, our price is quite competitive.

③如多买,可以有折扣。

If you buy more than 10 PCs, we will give you a 5% discount.

If your order is a sizable one, we could reconsider our price.

④同意客户还价。

OK, we agree to the price you asked for.

We decide to give you a 5% discount.

⑤说明同意还价的理由,比如,对方是新客户或者是经常光顾你店里的VIP客户等。

As you are our new customer, we decide to allow you a discount of 10%.

In view that you are our regular customer/VIP customer, we make an exception to offer you 15% off.

⑥说明折扣价已触底。

This is my last offer, anything lower than that will eat into our profits.

It is a good buy at this price.

You can't find a cheaper one.

That's the best I can do.

(4) 强调产品的卖点。

Please be assured that the quality of the goods you selected is quite good. The design is our best seller this year.

It's made of cotton, so it feels comfortable.

It's velvety and the color is brilliant.

The material is of good quality and holds color well.

This is pure silk and feels very soft.

As it fits you well, I think it's worthwhile to buy it.

(5) 关于产品尺码、颜色、护理等问题。

Which size should I choose?

Do you have the same blouse in a small size?

Do you have a large one?

Do you have a size in the middle?

I want to buy a pair of pants to match my shirt. Can you give me any advice?

Do you have this style in purple?

What colors do they come in besides red?

How about the handiwork? Are you sure it is well made?

Is it made of pure cotton?

What pattern do you prefer?

What material do you prefer?

This black dress looks attractive.

This color matches your coat.

I prefer a V-shaped collar to a turtleneck.

This windbreaker is perfect for spring.

Do you prefer low heel or high?

How about this skin?

The skin inside will fall off after some time, I'm afraid.

Is the skirt made of wool? I want a woolen one to keep me warm.

You can visit our store next Saturday. There will be some new arrivals.

How should I wash this woolen sweater?

I'm afraid it must be dry-cleaned.

It's better to wash it in cold water.

It's better to wash by hand.

Will it shrink after washing?

Will the color fade?

This leather jacket suits you well.

As it fits you well, I think it's worthwhile to buy it.

Is there anything else I can get for you?

It's been a pleasure doing business with you.

(6) 催下单。

We are writing to check if you have received our last quotation for leather bag dated May 28, 2017.

Please be assured that the quality of the goods you selected is quite good.

We would check the quality of the product and try our best to make sure you receive it in a satisfactory condition.

If you place your order, your item will be arranged within 24 – 48 hours and you'll get a courier number.

If you have any concern, please don't hesitate to let me know.

Anticipating your immediate response.

Awaiting your favorable reply.

(7) 催付款。

Thank you for your order No. XD 134 for jacket.

We noticed that you have not paid the order yet.

The special deal will be ending in 2 days.

If you make payment before the deadline, we will send you some nice gifts with your order.

The earlier you pay, the sooner shipment will be made.

If you have any problem with payment, please let us know.

Thank you for your cooperation.

(8) 告知缺货。

Right now we only have red, pink, black, white and yellow in stock. The green shoes you ordered are out of stock.

We don't have them in stock now.

Are you going to be ordering more?

We will contact the supplier to see when they will be available again.

Would you like other colors or other styles?

Would you like us to recommend you some other items with the same style/color?

We can give you a new item in better quality but at the same price.

We are looking forward to your early reply.

We are looking forward to your favorable reply.

Cross-border E-commerce English-Chinese Vocabulary（跨境电商英汉术语对照）

1. advisable	adj.		明智的
2. advise	v.		建议，告知
3. agreeable	adj.		惬意的，令人满意的
4. arrival	n.		到达物
5. available	adj.		有货的
6. bargain	v.		讨价还价
7. bargain	n.		便宜货
8. chest	n.		胸围
9. clear out stock			清货
10. complementary	adj.		补充的
11. contact	v.		联系
12. cotton	n.		棉
13. customer	n.		顾客
14. deal	n.		交易
15. discount	n.		折扣
16. dress	n.		连衣裙
17. dry clean			干洗
18. fade	v.		褪色
19. fit	v.		匹配
20. for your information			供你参考
21. garment care			衣服护理
22. hand wash			手洗
23. handiwork	n.		做工
24. have/keep something in stock			有货
25. heel	n.		（鞋、袜等的）后跟
26. height	n.		高度，身高
27. hesitate	v.		犹豫

28. hip		n.	臀围
29. in short supply			短缺
30. inch		n.	英寸
31. jacket		n.	夹克
32. L/large		adj.	大的，大号
33. length		n.	长度
34. M/medium		adj.	中间的，中等的，中号
35. machine washable			可机洗
36. match		v.	匹配
37. material		n.	材质
38. measurement		n.	尺寸
39. negotiable		adj.	可协商的
40. negotiate a price			议价
41. new arrival			新货
42. on clearance sale			清货
43. order		n.	订单
44. out of stock			无货
45. pattern		n.	花样，图案
46. payment		n.	支付
47. picture		n.	图片
48. place an order with sb. for sth.			向某人下订单
49. pound		n.	磅
50. purple		adj.	紫色的
51. qty/quantity		n.	数量
52. quality		n.	质量
53. quote		n.	报价
54. recommend		v.	推荐
55. replace		v.	代替
56. rinse		v.	冲洗，漂净
57. rub		v.	擦，揉；搓
58. S/small		adj.	小的，小号
59. sell at cost			按成本销售
60. shade		n.	阴凉处
61. shoulder		n.	肩宽
62. shrink		n.	缩水
63. silk		n.	丝绸
64. similar		adj.	相似的
65. size		n.	尺寸
66. skin		n.	皮

67. skirt		*n.*	短裙
68. sleeves length			袖长
69. stock		*n.*	库存
70. store		*n.*	商店
71. style		*n.*	风格，款式
72. supplier		*n.*	供应商
73. supply		*n. & v.*	供应
74. sweater		*n.*	毛衣
75. track		*v.*	跟踪
76. tracking number			快递追踪号
77. transaction		*n.*	交易
78. turtleneck		*n.*	高领
79. V-shaped collar			V 字领
80. waist		*n.*	腰围
81. weight		*n.*	重量
82. width		*n.*	宽度
83. windbreaker		*n.*	风衣
84. wool		*n.*	羊毛
85. woolen		*adj.*	羊毛的
86. worthwile		*adj.*	值得的
87. wring		*v.*	绞，拧
88. XL/extra large		*adj.*	特大号的，加大号的

Project 4

Delivery Service（发货服务）

Learning Aims（学习目标）

From learning this chapter, students will have a good command of the following skills.
1. Ability to write a shipping notification message to customers.
2. Ability to add tracking details online in English.
3. Ability to read and understand the logistics tracking information.
4. Ability to fill in the logistics surface.
5. Ability to write a notice of late shipment due to some reasons to customers.
6. Ability to write a notification message about the arrival of the goods.
7. Ability to write a notification message about late delivery of the goods.

Lead-in Situation（项目背景）

现在正值圣诞购物季，小熊贸易公司在跨境平台的店铺销售很好，订单出货频繁，已经连续几天加班。今日又有一批订单需要发货。跨境物流是跨境电商B2C交易中非常重要的一环，不但成本高、周期长，而且稍有差池，即会造成后续一系列不必要的麻烦，给客户造成很差的体验，继而影响店铺的评价和等级。该公司客服部发货专员Polly深知自己的认真仔细程度直接影响店铺服务指标，虽然很累还是打起精神开始进行发货操作。

Green-hand Guide（新手指南）

一、Cross-border Logistics Introduction（跨境物流介绍）

跨境物流目前主要有四类物流服务，分别是邮政物流、商业快递、专线物流和平台自有物流服务。

（一）邮政物流

邮政物流包括EMS，ePacket（e邮宝）和中国邮政航空大小包等。

1. EMS。

EMS，即Express Mail Service，也称特快专递邮件业务，是中国邮政速递物流与各国（地区）邮政合作开办的中国内地与中国港澳台或其他国家（地区）间寄送特快专递邮件的一项服务，它区别于商业快递的地方就在于它是

4　物流运费模板及包装

和其他国家（地区）的邮政合办，所以它在各国（地区）邮政、海关、航空等部门都享有优先处理权。

（1）资费标准、跟踪查询及体积、重量限制：卖家可在 EMS 官方网站查询这些信息。

（2）参考时效：EMS 国际快递投递时间通常是 3~8 个工作日（通关的时间除外）。因为不同国家和地区的邮政、海关处理时间有长有短，具体的承诺妥投时间要以官方网站公布的时间为准。

（3）优缺点：

优点——覆盖面广，邮政投递网络强大，以实重计费，不计算抛重，价格不像商业快递那么贵。适用于小件以及对时效性要求不是特别高的货物，可发敏感货物。有优先通关的权利，万一通关不过，货物可以免费运回国内。而其他快递在这种情况下都要收费。另外，不用提供商业发票就可以通关。

缺点——相对于商业快递来说，时效性没那么快。查询网站信息滞后，出现问题后只能做书面查询、查询时间比较长。另外，EMS 不能一票多件，大货价格偏高。

2. ePacket（e邮宝）。

ePacket 是中国邮政速递物流旗下的国际电子商务业务，目前可发美国、澳大利亚、英国、加拿大、法国和俄罗斯。

（1）资费标准、跟踪查询及参考时效：卖家可在 EMS 官方网站查询 ePacket 的资费标准。ePacket 业务不受理查单业务，也不提供邮件丢失、延误赔偿，所以要寄价值比较高的产品最好不要选择 ePacket。另外，中国邮政对 ePacket 业务是没有承诺时效的。

（2）体积、重量限制：

1）单件最高限重 2kg。

2）最大尺寸：单件长、宽、高加起来不超过 90cm，最长一边不超过 60cm。圆卷货物直径的两倍和长度加起来不超过 104cm，长度不超过 90cm。

3）最小尺寸：单件长度不小于 14cm，宽度不小于 11cm。圆卷货物直径的两倍和长度加起来不小于 17 cm，长度不小于 11cm。

3. 中国邮政航空大小包。

（1）中国邮政航空大包。

中国邮政航空大包，即 China Post Air Parcel，俗称航空大包或中邮大包，可寄达全球200 多个国家（地区），价格低廉，通关能力强，卖家要发对时效性要求不太高而且比较重的货物时可选择大包，性价比较高。卖家可上网查询相关资费标准、体积和重量限制，跟踪物流信息。

优点——以首重 1kg、续重 1kg 的计费方式结算，且不计算体积重量，没有偏远附加费，价格比 EMS 低，和商业快递相比有绝对的价格优势。可通达全球大部分国家和地区，而且操作简单。

缺点——限重 30kg，部分国家限重 10kg。妥投速度慢，查询信息更新慢。

（2）中国邮政航空小包。

中国邮政航空小包，即 China Post Air Mail，俗称中邮小包、空邮小包、航空小包，是重量在 2kg 以下，外包装长、宽、高之和小于 90cm，且最长边小于 60cm，通过邮政空邮服务寄往国外的小邮包，也可称为国际小包。它分为中国邮政平常小包和挂号小包，两者的区别在于挂号小包能在中国邮政官方网站上实时跟踪邮包在全球大部分目的国（地区）的实时状态，而中国邮政平常小包，亦称平邮小包，不受理查询，只能通过面单条码用电话查询邮包在国内的状态。

优点——运费便宜,性价比高,通关能力强,派送网络世界各地都有,覆盖面非常广。另外,能邮寄的物品种类多,限制没有商业快递那么多。

缺点——有限重,有的国家物品运送时间长。因为很多国家不支持全程跟踪、邮政官方网站只能跟踪国内部分,卖家需要借助社会公司的网站或者是登录寄达国(地区)的查询网来进行跟踪。

(二)商业快递

商业快递的特点是速度快、服务好、专业、高效、价格比较高,适用于货值比较高、买家要求比较高的商品。

1. 荷兰 TNT 快递。

(1)资费标准、跟踪查询及参考时效:TNT 的运费包括基本运费和燃油附加费,后者每月都会变动。卖家可在 TNT 官方网站上查询燃油附加费并进行跟踪查询。一般货物全程时效是 3~5 天,经济型时效是 5~7 天。

(2)体积重量限制:单件包裹不超过 70kg,长、宽、高三条边分别不超过 2.4m、1.5m 和 1.2m,货物体积重量超过实际重量的情况下按体积重量收费,体积重量的算法为长(cm)×宽(cm)×高(cm)÷5 000。

(3)优缺点。

优点——速度快,通关能力强,提供报关代理服务,网络全,可免费、及时、准确地追踪查询货物。

缺点——对所运货物限制比较多,价格较高,计算体积重量。

2. 美国 UPS。

UPS 历史悠久,是世界上最大的快递承运商和包裹递送公司之一,全球总部位于美国的亚特兰大。

(1)资费标准、跟踪查询及参考时效:卖家可在 UPS 官方网站上查询资费标准和跟踪查询,参考派送时间一般为 2~4 个工作日。

(2)体积重量限制:每个包裹最大重量为 70kg,最大长度为 270cm,最大尺寸为长度+[2×(高度+宽度)]=330 cm。如果包裹超过这个重量和尺寸,每个包裹最多收取一次超重超长附加费 378 元。

(3)优缺点:

优点——速度快、服务好、可在线发货、全国 109 个城市提供上门取货服务。寄往美洲有优势,特别是美国,最快 24 小时就可送达,查询网站信息更新快。

缺点——对所运货物限制比较多,运费较贵,计算体积重量。

3. DHL。

(1)资费标准、跟踪查询及参考时效:卖家可在 DHL 官方网站上查询资费标准并进行跟踪查询,计算体积重量,体积重量的算法为长(cm)×宽(cm)×高(cm)÷5 000。客户交货之后第二天开始计算参考时效,1~2 个工作日后就可上网查询信息,参考妥投时效为 3~7 个工作日(不包括通关时间)。

(2)体积重量限制:寄往大多数国家的单件包裹的重量不超过 70kg,最长边不超过 1.2m。

（3）优缺点：

优点——速度快，特别是寄往西欧和北美，一般2~4个工作日便可送达，网站信息查询更新快。

缺点——对所运货物限制比较多，价格较贵，计算体积重量。

4. FedEx。

FedEx全名为Federal Express，也称联邦快递，分为中国联邦快递优先型服务和中国联邦快递经济型服务两种。

（1）资费标准、跟踪查询及参考时效：卖家可在FedEx官方网站上查询资费标准并进行跟踪查询，计算体积重量，体积重量的算法为长（cm）×宽（cm）×高（cm）÷5 000。中国联邦快递优先型服务的正常时效为2~5个工作日，中国联邦快递经济型服务的正常时效为4~6个工作日。

（2）体积重量限制：货物单件的最长边不超过274cm，最长边和其他两边长度的两倍不超过330cm，总重量不超过300kg。可一票多件，其中每件不超过68kg，超过68kg的要提前预约。

优点——适合寄送大件，速度快，网站查询信息更新快。

缺点——对所运货物限制比较多，价格较贵，计算体积重量。

5. SF Express。

SF Express也称顺丰速递，最初以中国大陆、中国港澳台为主要服务范围，目前已开通美、日、韩、新马泰、越南、澳大利亚等国家的快递服务。

（1）资费标准、跟踪查询：卖家可在SF Express官方网站上查询资费标准并进行跟踪查询，计算体积重量，体积重量的算法为长（cm）×宽（cm）×高（m）÷6 000。

（2）优缺点。

优点——国内服务网点分布广、服务好。

缺点——开通的国家线路少。

注：国际物流方式多种多样，各有其优缺点（表4-1），所以在实际工作中应选择适合产品特点的物流方式。

表4-1　国际物流主要承运公司选择

承运人	费用	运输周期	货物查询	适用商品	运费计算	燃油附加费
EMS	一般	一般	可查	时间要求不高，体积大，注重运费成本	"直达"只算包装后的实重；"非直达"实重和体积运费从高	无
FedEx、DHLTNT、UPS	高	短	可查	价值高，时间要求高，服务质量高	实重和体积运费从高	每月更新
ChinaPost HKPost	低	长	可查	时间要求不高，货物价值低，体积较大	只算包装后的实重	无

(三) 专线物流

1. 燕文专线 Special Line—YW。

燕文专线是北京燕文物流公司旗下的一项国际物流业务。包裹重量小于 2kg，方形包裹至少有一面的长度大于 14cm，宽度大于 9cm，但长、宽、高之和小于 90cm，最长一边长度小于 60cm；圆柱形包裹直径的 2 倍与长度之和大于 17cm、小于 104cm，长度大于 10cm、小于 90cm。正常情况下可 16~35 天到达目的地，但在节假日、特殊天气、政策调整或偏远地区等情况下是 35~60 天到达目的地。

2. 俄速通 Ruston。

俄速通是黑龙江俄速通国际物流有限公司提供的中俄航空小包专线服务，递送范围覆盖俄罗斯全境，全程可追踪，资费标准为 85 元/kg + 8 元挂号费。在正常情况下 15~25 天可到达目的地，在特殊情况下 30 天内到达目的地。

3. 中东专线 Aramex。

中东专线是中东地区的国际快递巨头。标准运费包括基本运费和燃油附加费，价格计算方式为

邮费 =（首重价格 + 续重价格 × 续重数量）+ 燃油附加费 × 折扣

香港 Aramex 首重为 0.5kg，单个包裹的重量限制为 30kg；广州 Aramex 单个包裹的重量无限制。体积重量超过实际重量需按照体积重量计费，体积重量的算法为长（cm）× 宽（cm）× 高（cm）÷5 000，包裹参考时效为 6~10 天。

4. 芬兰邮政。

芬兰邮政是由速卖通和芬兰邮政合作推出的针对 2kg 以下小件物品的特快物流服务，运送范围为俄罗斯和白俄罗斯全境邮局可达区域，分为经济型小包和挂号小包。

经济型小包运费 = 配送服务费 × 包裹实际重量

挂号小包运费 = 配送服务费 × 包裹实际重量 + 挂号服务费

包裹寄出后大部分在 35 天内可以到达。

5. 中俄专线 SPSR。

中俄专线是俄罗斯最优秀的商业物流公司之一，SPSR 提供的运送范围为俄罗斯全境。单件包裹重量不超过 15kg，体积不超过 60cm × 60cm × 60cm，单边长度不超过 60cm。其资费标准与中邮航空小包一致，包裹参考时效为 14~32 天。

（四）平台自有物流——速卖通物流服务

1. 认识无忧物流 AliExpress。

AliExpress 是速卖通及菜鸟网络联合推出的速卖通官方物流服务，为速卖通卖家提供稳定的国内揽收、国际配送、物流详情追踪、物流纠纷处理及售后赔付的一站式物流解决方案。

2. AliExpress 的优势。

AliExpress 的优势体现在以下几个方面。

（1）渠道稳定、时效快。

1）菜鸟网络与优质物流商合作，搭建覆盖全球的物流配送网络。

2）业内领先的智能分担系统，根据目的国、品类、重量自动匹配最优物流方案。

（2）运费优惠。
1）重点国家运费约为市场价格的 80%~90%，只发一件也有折扣。
2）使用支付宝在线支付运费。
（3）操作简单。
1）一键选择 AliExpress 即可完成运费模板设置。
2）出单后发货到国内仓库即可，深圳、广州、义乌等重点城市免费上门揽收。
（4）平台承担售后。
1）物流纠纷无须卖家响应，直接由平台介入，核实物流状态并判责。
2）因物流原因导致的纠纷、DSR 低分不计入卖家账号考核。
（5）平台承担物流纠纷退款。
物流原因导致的纠纷退款由平台承担，标准物流赔付上限为 800 元人民币，优先物流赔付上限为 1 200 元人民币。

3. AliExpress 的使用流程（图 4-1）。

图 4-1

4. AliExpress 线上发货操作。
（1）认识线上发货。
线上发货是由速卖通及菜鸟网络联合多家优质第三方物流商打造的物流服务体系。卖家使用线上发货需要在速卖通后台在线下载物流订单，物流商上门揽收后（或卖家自寄至物流商仓库），卖家可在线支付运费并在线发起物流维权。阿里巴巴作为第三方将全程监督物流商服务质量，保障卖家权益。其基本流程如图 4-2 所示。

图 4-2

（2）线上发货的优势。
1）卖家保护政策。
A. 平台网规认可。使用线上发货且成功入库的包裹，买卖双方均可在速卖通后台（订单详情页面）查看物流追踪信息，且平台网规认可。后续卖家遇到投诉，无须再提交发货订单等相关物流追踪信息证明。
B. 规避物流低分，提高账号表现。每个月进行卖家服务等级评定时，使用线上发货的订单，因物流原因导致的低分可抹除。
C. 物流问题赔偿保障。阿里巴巴作为第三方将全程监督物流商服务质量，保障卖家权益。卖家可针对丢包、货物破损、运费争议等物流问题在线发起投诉并获得赔偿（仅国际小包物流方案支持）。
2）运费低于市场价，支付更方便。
A. 可享受速卖通专属合约运费。低于市场价，只发一件也可享受折扣。
B. 在线用支付宝付运费。国际支付宝账户中未结汇美元也能付运费，还能下载运费电子账单对账。

3)渠道稳定,时效快。

A. 渠道稳定。直接和中国邮政等物流商对接,安全可靠。

B. 时效快。平台数据显示,线上发货时效快,妥投时效高于线下。

C. 物流商承诺运达时间。因物流商原因在承诺时间内未妥投而引起的限时达纠纷赔款由物流商承担。

二、Attention to Problems in Cross-border Logistics Operation(跨境物流操作注意问题)

(1)所有待发货产品在包装之前一定要进行仔细的检查,确保所有产品无色差、无破损、无瑕疵,避免后续的"货不对版"纠纷。

(2)在包装时,要考虑到产品是否为易碎品。若产品是易碎品,则需使用气泡膜进行加固包装,否则在运输途中受到挤压、碰撞等会造成破碎,后期会产生"货不对版"纠纷。

(3)通常情况下不同的物流方式所使用的物流面单有所区别,以"中国邮政挂号小包"为例,图4-3所示是"中国邮政挂号小包一体化面单",条码下面方框里的内容是需要填写的,包括产品名称、数量、重量以及申报价值,而其他信息其实是系统自动生成的。

图4-3

(4)卖家常用跨境物流服务提供商。

1)China Post Small Package by Air 中国航空邮政小包。

2)ePacket e邮宝。

3)China Post Registered Air Mail 中国邮政挂号小包。

4)Hong Kong Post Air Mail 香港邮政挂号小包。

5)Special Line—YW 燕文航空挂号小包。

6)4PX Singapore Post OM Pro 4PX 新邮经济小包。

7)SF Express 顺丰速运。

Mission Implementation(任务实施)

Task 1 Off-line Shipping(线下发货)

发货专员Polly首先对所有待发货的服装进行一一检查,确保所有衣服无色差、无破损、无瑕疵；接着根据衣服的尺寸，选择合适的包装袋进行包装；然后填写物流面单，将物流面单贴到产品的包装袋上。以下是某个订单的信息，请你帮 Polly 据此填入物流一体化面单中：

订单编号：82049912345678

物流方式：中国邮政小包

客户名称：Graciela Quintana

客户地址：Raulmuriel 1121，ushuaia，Tierra del Fuego，Argentina

客户邮编：9410

客户联系电话：542901123456

国家：阿根廷

产品信息：

产品型号	产品名称规格	数量	重量	申报价值
CN040－h1－s	Kids clothes，US Size 7，Color red	2	0.4kg	$10

根据上述订单信息将相关内容填入物流一体化面单中（图 4－4）。

图 4－4　物流一体化面单

Task 2　Add Tracking Details Online（添加线上的追踪信息）

完成包装，填完物流面单后，发货专员 Polly 根据相关信息填写发货信息。

步骤 1：按照如图 4－5 所示选择物流方案。

步骤 2：按照如图 4－6 所示创建物流订单。

Notes（解析）

（1）在速卖通平台上有中文操作界面，也可采用英语操作界面。

（2）订单履行进程：Place Order（下单）＜＜＜＜＜Pay Success（支付成功）＜＜＜Shipment（发货）。此例中，"Shipment"为灰色条目，表示发货尚未完成。正如 Status（状态）上所显示，Awaiting Order Shipment（等待订单发货）。

（3）速卖通平台上有两种发货方式：一种为卖家自己找货代公司发货；另一种是货发速卖通的签约货代，进行线上发货（Online Shipping）。此例为货发速卖通签约货代。

图 4-5　速卖通线上发货操作之选择物流方案

图 4-6　速卖通线上发货操作之创建物流订单

（4）Ship From 发货地：既可以选择中国，有海外仓备货的也可以选择海外。

（5）Tracking No. 跟踪号：必须填写真实的货运跟踪号，填写虚假运单号会受到平台处罚。

（6）若只发出部分货物，发货状态需选择"部分发货（Part Shipment）"，并告知客户。

Task 3　Writing a Shipping Notification（撰写发货通知）

线上填写发货信息后，发货专员 Polly 撰写发货通知，告知客户货物已发出。

Hello Dawood,

We are happy to tell you we have dispatched your order!

You can track its progress with the following tracking No.: RM725 132179CN. It usually takes about 25 days for your order arriving, but as this is the shopping season, the logistics companies are very busy and some orders may take slightly longer to arrive.

> If you have any question or problem, contact us directly for help.
> Have a nice day!
> Polly

Notes（解析）

在撰写发货通知时，需要注意发货通知的语言风格。有些店铺的风格会正式些、书面化些；而大部分网络店铺都会比较亲切，用语口语化。在上一封信中，可以发现邮件的招呼语用了 hello，称谓用了客户的个性化名字，而发货通知的句子则用了主动态，这样显得更为亲切。

Task 4　Tracking Logistics Information Online（追踪线上物流信息）

货物发出一段时间后，浙江爱丽服装有限公司物流部发货专员王力开始追踪物流信息，了解货物的运输情况。

步骤1：进入物流查询网站 www.17track.net。
步骤2：输入货运跟踪号。
步骤3：点击"查询"。

Notes（解析）

从物流追踪信息中我们可以看到货物运输的不同状态：

Not Found 查不到———可能是货物刚发出，物流信息还没及时更新，或者该单号是虚假的。

In Transit 运输途中———一切正常。

Pick Up 到达待取———货物已经到达目的地，等待收件人去领取。

Undelivered 投递失败———由于地址有误或者无法联系到收件人，货物无法投递。

Delivered 成功签收。

Alert 可能异常———货物可能丢失。

Expired 运输过久———由于物流障碍，货物一直在运输途中。

Task 5　Writing a Notification about the Arrival of the Goods（撰写货物到达的通知）

发货专员 Polly 在查询物流信息后，发现一批订单的货物即将到达目的国家（地区），于是他需要群发给客户邮件，告知这一信息。

> Dear ×××,
> We have tracked the logistic information for your parcel. It shows your parcel will soon arrive at your end. Hope you would be satisfied with our goods.
> Have a lovely day.
> ×××

Notes（解析）

（1）撰写此封信的目的在于提醒客户货物即将到达，请不要忘记取货。

（2）为客户查询物流状态时，如果物流状态显示为 In Transit，且物流信息很长时间没有更新，说明运输遇到了问题，到货时间可能会延误，一定要及时告知客户，以减少可能存在的未到货纠纷。

物流服务常用电邮模板示例 Logistic Service E-mail Model

E-mail 1

Dear ×××,

We have tracked the logistic information and it hasn't been updated due to the problem of system. But don't worry, the goods are in transit. Perhaps you will receive the goods a few days later. Please wait with patience.

Have a lovely day.

×××

E-mail 2

Dear friend,

We sincerely regret that you've not yet received your shipment. As per the tracking information, your item is on the way to your country, which left China on May 12, 2017.

Tracking No: ××××××

Status: ××××××

Shipped Date: ××××××

Could you please kindly wait for some more days? Standard shipping times are approximately 7 – 15 business days. We will help you trace your shipment at our end and keep you updated.

Your satisfaction is our utmost priority; please contact us if you have any concern.

We apologize for the inconvenience. Your understanding is greatly appreciated.

Best regards!

Walker

E-mail 3

Hi, friend,

We are sorry to hear that. Could you please kindly check with your other family members or neighbors?

If you still do not find the goods, please kindly help us go to the local post for lost claim.

You just need to send us the claim copy. Then we will compensate you right a way after that and then talk with the post against your claim at our end.

Thanks,

Walker

E-mail 4

Dear friend,

We sincerely regret that you haven't yet received your shipment. As per the tracking informa-

tion, your item is on the way to your country, which left China on ××××××, 2017.
Tracking No：××××××
Status：××××××
Shipped Date：××××××
Could you please kindly wait for some more days? We are sorry that the delay is due to the bad weather/war/peak season issue. If it still doesn't arrive at your place in 15 days, we will send you a new one or issue the full refund to you.
Best regards!
Walker

E-mail 5

Dear friend,
We are sorry to find that your item is returning to us due to wrong address.
Can you tell me a new address?
We are happy to arrange the new shipment to you, but could you please kindly help us cover the freight cost?
Please kindly notice that we can only cover the freight cost caused by wrong items, lost items as well as poor quality.
Hopefully you can understand.

E-mail 6

Dear friend,
Thank you for your message about non-updated logistic information.
After checking with our forwarder, we are informed that your parcel is still kept in ChinaPost warehouse due to labor shortage, as we are in Chinese New Year. Luckily, we can expect the updated information within 3 days.
If you have any question, please contact us. We are always at your service.
Sorry to cause your inconvenience.
Steven

跨境物流常用句示例
1. 告知客户货（具体）已发出。
Your parcel of kids clothes has been sent with tracking No. RM725132179CN.
2. 告知客户如何跟踪自己的订单。
You can check delivery status on website http://www.17track.net/en.
3. 告知客户物流所需的大概时间。
You will receive the parcel in 15 – 25 days.
4. 告知客户如果发生问题，该如何处理。

If you have any question, contact us directly.

Cross-border E-commerce English-Chinese Vocabulary（跨境电商英汉术语对照）

1. dispatch	v.		发货
2. send	v.		发送
3. deliver	v.		发运
4. ship	v.		发运
5. parcel	n.		包裹
6. add./address	n.		地址
7. arrival	n.		到达
8. arrive	v.		到达
9. at one's end			在某一方
10. delivery status			运送状态
11. expire	v.		期满，到期
12. in transit			运输途中
13. logistic	adj.		物流的，后勤的
14. notification	n.		通知
15. off-line shipping			线下发货
16. order No.			订单号
17. P. O. BOX			邮箱
18. sender	n.		寄件人
19. ship to			收货人
20. shopping season			销售旺季
21. shortage	n.		缺乏，不足
22. standard shipping time			标准运输时间
23. TEL/telephone	n.		电话
24. total gross weight			总毛重
25. track	v.		追踪
26. transaction	n.		交易
27. val./value	n.		货值
28. zip	n.		邮编
29. not found			查询不到
30. pick up			到达待取
31. undelivered			投递失败
32. delivered			成功签收
33. alert			货物异常
34. expired			运输过久

Project 5

After-sale Service (售后客服)

Learning Aims (学习目标)

From learning this chapter, students can reply to customers' mails from Information Center on Cross-border E-commerce Platform, deal with after-sale services and communicate effectively.

1. Understand the common customer problems in the after-sale phase.

2. Exercise the ability to understand the core information of the buyer's letter.

3. To master the after-sale communicating skills related to payment delay, shipping problems, customs inspection, product damage, feedback requirements, etc.

Lead-in Situation (项目背景)

小熊贸易公司在速卖通平台上开立了一家童装店,客服专员 Peter 和 Anne 专门负责客户的售后服务。主管告诉他们客户评价和纠纷会影响店铺的服务等级,从而影响店铺的曝光和资源流量,是非常重要的考核指标。因此,如何避免及处理纠纷、获得好评价、提高卖家服务等级是他们跨境客服专员售后工作的重点。要想做好客服工作,上岗工作前请先学习平台规则。

Cross-border E-commerce Platform Rules (跨境电商平台规则)

跨境电商平台考核卖家服务等级的指标有:DSR 物流服务、DSR 商品描述、成交不卖率、退单率、好评率、货不对版仲裁提起率、货不对版仲裁有责率、DSR 卖家服务纠纷提起率等。平台纠纷通常容易在两方面产生:买家未收到货而产生的纠纷(未到货),买家收到货但是货物与产品描述不符所导致的纠纷(货不对版)。

以速卖通平台为例,在交易过程中,难免会遇到买家要求退货退款情况。一旦买家提起该申请,即进入纠纷阶段,须买卖双方协商解决。速卖通纠纷处理流程如下。

一、**Buyer Files Only Refund/Return & Refund Application** (买家提起退款/退货退款申请)

1. 买家提交纠纷的原因:

(1) 未收到货。

(2) 收到的货物与约定不符。

(3) 买家自身原因。

2. 买家提交退款申请时间:可以在卖家全部发货 10 天后申请退款(若卖家设置的限时

达时间小于 5 天，则买家可以在卖家全部发货后立即申请退款）。

3. 买家端操作：在提交速卖通纠纷页面中，买家可以看到选项"Only Refund"和"Return & Refund"，选择"Only Refund"就可以提交仅退款申请，选择"Return & Refund"就可以提交退货退款申请。提交退货退款/仅退款申请后，买家需要描述问题与解决方案以及上传证据。买家提交纠纷后，平台纠纷"小二"会在 7 天内（包含第 7 天）介入处理。

二、Transaction Negotiation Between Buyers and Sellers（买卖双方交易协商）

买家提起退货/退款申请后，需要卖家的确认，卖家可以在纠纷列表页面中看到所有的纠纷订单。快速筛选区域展示关键纠纷状态："纠纷处理中"，"买家已提交纠纷，等待您确认"，"等待您确认收货"。对于卖家未响应过的纠纷，点击"接受"或"拒绝并提供方案"按钮进入纠纷详情，页面如图 5-1 所示。

图 5-1　纠纷订单处理页面示例

进入速卖通纠纷详情页面（图 5-2），卖家可以看到买家提起纠纷的时间、原因、证据以及买家提供的协商方案等信息。当买家提起纠纷后，请卖家在买家提起纠纷的 5 天内接受或拒绝买家提出的纠纷，若逾期未响应，系统会自动根据买家提出的退款金额执行。建议您在协商阶段积极与买家沟通。

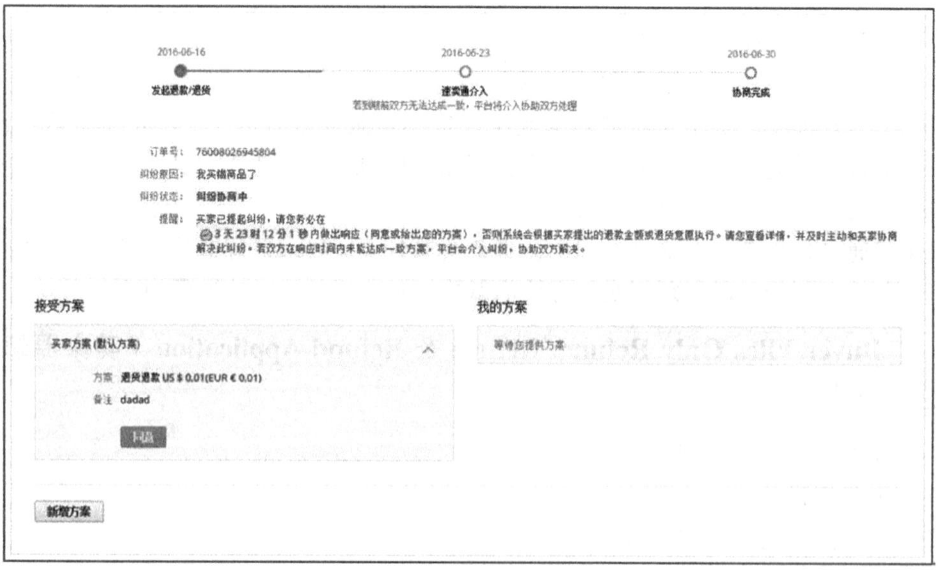

图 5-2　纠纷详情页面

卖家可以：

（一）同意协商方案

买家提起的退款申请有以下两种类型：

（1）仅退款：卖家接受时会提示卖家确认退款方案；若同意退款申请，则退款协议达成，款项会按照双方达成一致的方案执行（图5-3）。

图5-3 同意买家退款方案页面

（2）退货退款：若卖家接受，则需要卖家确认收货地址，默认卖家注册时候填写的地址（地址需要全部以英文来填写）；若地址不正确，则点击"修改收货地址"。

（二）新增或修改证据

新增或修改证据页面如图5-4所示。

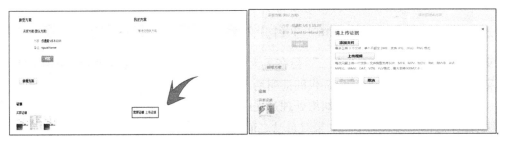

图5-4 新增或修改证据页面

（三）增加或修改协商方案

买家和卖家最多可提供两个互斥方案（方案一提交了退货退款方案后，方案二默认只能选仅退款不退货的方案），如图5-5，图5-6所示。

图 5-5　修改方案页面

图 5-6　方案修改内容页面

(四) 删除方案/证据

买家和卖家都可以对自己提交的方案或举证进行删除（图 5-7、图 5-8）。

图 5-7　证据删除页面

图 5-8　方案删除页面

三、Platform Involvement（平台介入协商）

买家提交纠纷后，纠纷"小二"会在 7 天内（包含第 7 天）介入处理。速卖通平台会参看案件情况以及双方协商阶段提供的证明给出方案。买家、卖家在纠纷详情页面可以看到买家、卖家、平台三方的方案。纠纷处理过程中，纠纷原因、方案、举证均可随时独立修改（在案件结束之前，买家、卖家如果对自己之前提供的方案、证据等不满意，则可以随时进行修改）。买家、卖家如果接受对方或者平台给出的方案，则可以点击接受此方案，此时双方对同一个方案达成一致，纠纷完成。在纠纷完成赔付状态中，买、卖双方不能够再协商。

四、The Return Process（退货流程）

如果卖家和买家达成退款又退货的协议，则买家必须在 10 天内将货物发出（否则款项会打给卖家）。买家退货并填写退货运单号后，卖家有 30 天的确认收货时间，如果未收到货物或对收到的货物不满，则可以直接将订单提交给纠纷平台。纠纷平台相关部门会联系双方跟进处理（图5-9，图5-10）。（注：买家退货后，卖家需要在30天内确认收货或提起纠纷，若逾期未操作，则默认为卖家收货，执行退款操作。）

图5-9 协议达成买方退货页面

图5-10 卖家放弃退货页面

若买家已经退货，填写了退货单号，则需要等待卖家确认（图5-11）。

图5-11 买家退货页面

卖家需在30天内确认收到退货：

（1）若确认收到退货，并同意退款，则点击"确定"按钮（图5-12），速卖通会退款给买家（卖家操作页面如图5-12所示）。

卖家确认收货，纠纷完成。

（2）若卖家在接近30天的时间内没有收到退货，或收到的退货有问题，卖家可以点击"升级纠纷"提交至平台进行纠纷裁决（操作页面如图5-13所示），平台会在2个工作日内介入处理，卖家可以在纠纷页面查看状态及进行响应。平台裁决期间，卖家也可以点击

图 5-12　卖家确认收到退货页面

"撤销仲裁"以撤销纠纷裁决（操作页面如图 5-14 所示）。

图 5-13　卖家提交纠纷升级页面

图 5-14　卖家撤销纠纷仲裁页面

（3）若 30 天内卖家未进行任何操作，即未确认收货，未提交纠纷裁决，则系统会默认卖家已收到退货，自动退款给买家。海外仓本地退货，双方达成一致退货后，若订单支持本地退货，平台会展示退货地址。确认收货后，纠纷完成。

五、AliExpress Logistics Dispute Settlement（无忧物流纠纷）

使用速卖通无忧物流发货的订单，买家发起未收到货纠纷后，卖家无须响应，直接由平台介入核实物流状态并判责。非物流问题导致的纠纷，仍然需要卖家自行处理。

Green-hand Guide（新手指南）

一、Basic Principles of Dispute Settlement（纠纷处理的基本原则）

1. 每日查看，及时响应：纠纷的响应时间是 5 天，如果超过 5 天不回应，响应超时，直接退款。不管这个纠纷是不是棘手，如果时间只剩下 2 天，先拒绝掉。

2. 一切以店铺安全为前提，理智处理：纠纷里面物流原因直接决定商品的 DSR，产品质量纠纷直接决定货不对版纠纷提起率，如果你的某个类目分数都快要超标关掉了，你却告诉我"这个质量纠纷我一定要赢！"是非常不理性的。请理智处理，记住店铺安全第一。

3. 客服有义务将纠纷损失降到最低：对于每个月纠纷退款的损失，在某种程度上客服有权利降低到最小，比如物流承诺运达先退款了，但是客户收到后，可以留言客户部分退还。

5 客服与订单管理

二、Dispute Types and Handling Skills（纠纷类型及处理技巧）

纠纷类型总体来讲分为三类：物流纠纷、质量纠纷、恶意纠纷。下面分别针对相关情况，列举客户沟通邮件范例。

（一）物流纠纷

1. 无物流信息，处理思路：ERP 查询是否发货，如果已发货，则是物流信息更新迟滞。

● 缺货未发。

Dear Valued Customer,
Really sorry for the inconvenience, the item you buy is out of stock. New stock maybe needs 2 – 3 weeks to arrive. We can refund you the full money soon. Usually AliExpress will deal with it with in 3 – 5 working days.
Once you receive the money, please give me 5 – star good feedback. Next time when you buy from my store, we can give you VIP price, and do better after-sale for you.
If you have any problem, leave me message here. We will reply to you within 24 hours.
Best wishes

● 发货后信息未更新。

Dear Valued Customer,
Really sorry for the inconvenience. Just because we ship the package to AliExpress Warehouse yesterday, so they need some time to deal with it, and will update the tracking info on website soon. We will send you the tracking website. You can track it by yourself.
Really hope you can help me cancel the dispute first. If you still cannot see the tracking info updated, you can open dispute again.
Wait for your kindly reply!
Best wishes

2. 有物流信息。

• 货物在途中,一直没出国(大促活动期间)。

Dear Valued Customer,

Really sorry for the inconvenience. In fact we have already shipped it to AliExpress Warehouse. You can track it on the Internet. It shows shipment information received.

Really hope you can help me cancel the dispute first. We have asked my logistics company to check it for you. If they have any update, we will leave you message ASAP.

Best Wishes

• 没出国显示退回(带电未过安检)。

Dear Valued Customer,

Really sorry for the inconvenience. Thank you for your business. Your order has been returned to us by the Customs. Just because the power bank is difficult to pass the customs. We need refund you full money. Wait for your quick reply. Thanks a lot!

Also hope you can give me 5 – star good feedback. Hope you can forgive me for the uncontrollable shipping problem. Next time we can apply the VIP price and better after-sale for you from my company.

Best wishes

• 海关扣关(留言分类一篇有提到具体的原因)。

Dear Valued Customer,

Really sorry for the inconvenience. I just received an e-mail from our logistics company, and I track the package on the website. Your parcel arrived at your country customs, waiting for you to finish the customs clearance.

Really hope you can help me cancel the dispute first. If you have any problem, leave me message here. We will reply to you within 24 hours.

Best wishes

• 货到目的国家(地区)1~2个月未更新。

Dear Valued Customer,

Sorry for the inconvenience. We just help you track the parcel. In fact the package already arrived at your country at the date ***.

And I have extended the delivery date by *** days for you. So never worry that the protection time is running out. We hope you can try to give a call to your local post office, ask them to help you track it. Also China post is really a little slow. Hope you understand this situation.

If you still don't receive it within ** days, we can apply the refund from my company for you. Do not worry about that. We are the honest seller, so hope you can be a little patient, help us cancel the dispute first. Just because of the AliExpress Shopping Festival, there are so many parcels to be shipped.

Anyway if you have any problem, leave me message here. We will reply to you within 24 hours.

Best wishes

- 买家说未收到货，目的国家（地区）显示妥投成功。

Dear Valued Customer,

Sorry for the inconvenience. In fact we just track the parcel, Which shows it was delivered successfully. But you said you had not got it yet. We hope you can contact your local post office. We can send you all the proof to show that we've sent the package according to your order address, and we can give you the evidence of my logistics company.

Anyway, if you have any problem, leave me message here. We will reply to you within 24 hours.

Best wishes

- 卖家私自更改物流方式。

Dear Valued Customer,

Sorry for the inconvenience. I just help you track the parcel, Which shows it was delivered successfully. Since you are already my VIP customer, I hope you can help me cancel the dispute. Next time we need confirm with you carefully when we need change the shipping way. Sorry for that mistake.

And I just applied the best after-sale for you. We can give you a discount $8 when you buy in my store next time. Anyway, if you have any problem, leave me message here. We will reply to you within 24 hours.

Best wishes

（二）质量纠纷

- 描述不符（尺寸、颜色、语言、重量等）。

思路：看不符点是否影响客户的使用；要尽量减少损失，并且立刻修改 Listing。比如：产品包装不符，完全可以正常使用。

Dear Valued Customer,

Sorry for the inconvenience. Just because this product has been updated nowadays, we only changed the package. In fact, all the functions are the same as before. I hope you can understand, and you can test it. Also I see you have bought it before in my store.

Thanks for your remind. I just talked with my boss. We can give you a VIP price next time.

Best wishes

- 不能工作（针对电子产品）。

思路：电子产品尽可能要求客户提供照片和视频。

Dear Valued Customer,

Sorry for the inconvenience. We hope you can shoot a very short video (To send a video link is also OK) or some pictures to my e-mail：******. Remember to write the title such as：Order NO. *******, so we can find it more easily in my store.

Once we receive your e-mail, we will let my engineer check it for you, and reply to you soon.

Best wishes

- 销售假货（提交品牌授权书即可）。

  思路：前提是所经营的产品确实为正品，直接提供品牌授权证书或者查询网址。

Dear Valued Customer,

Sorry for the inconvenience. In fact, all the *** Brand products in my store are 100% original. We have been authorized by **** Company. Try to check the picture in the attachment. As you can see that we are the top brand seller in AliExpress. So we can guarantee the product quality for my customers. We hope you can help me cancel the dispute.

Best wishes

- 货物短装（最好直接补发）。

Dear Valued Customer

Sorry for the inconvenience. Maybe my warehouse made a mistake, but anyway we hope you can send me some pictures for check. Once we confirm with my warehouse and logistics company, we will send you a new one.

After we give you a new tracking number, you can track it after 2~3 days. I hope you can help me cancel the dispute if we send you a new one. Wait for your kindly reply.

Best wishes

- 收到退货（7天无理由本地退货）。

Dear Valued Customer,

Sorry for the inconvenience. If you really do not like it, I hope you can help me pack it well, and put all the accessories in box. Because my Russian Warehouse needs to check it carefully when they received it. I hope you can understand.

Once they received it, we can refund you the full money, and I hope you can give me a 5-star good feedback.

Thanks a lot.

- 赠品纠纷（答应的赠品没寄）。

Dear Valued Customer,

Sorry for the inconvenience. In fact, we have told my warehouse already, but they forget to put the gift in the package. They are really sorry for that. If it is OK, I hope you can help me cancel the dispute first. We can give you a discount $3 next time when you buy in my store. Or we can send you a free gift in the next package. I will pack it by myself. So never worry about that. Wait for your kindly reply.

Best wishes

（三）恶意纠纷

- 质量问题恶意纠纷（最常见的就是不工作）。

思路：只要涉及电子产品不工作，一定要让买家先提供视频。

Dear Valued Friend,

Really sorry for that inconvenience. We wonder if you can shoot a very short video (To send a video link is also OK) to my e-mail: ****. Remember to write the title: Order NO. ************

Once we receive your e-mail, we will let my engineer check it for you, find the good solution, and reply to you soon.

Best wishes

- 邮局收费恶意纠纷（提供发票让国外朋友确认）。

思路：客户提供照片以确认。

Dear Valued Friend,

Really sorry for that inconvenience. In fact, we send you by China Post. As I know, usually this way never need charge extra fee. Maybe it is your local post office policy, because we have already paid the shipping fee for you. I hope you can send me a picture of the bill.

Once we received the picture, we will reply to you soon, and help you solve the problem ASAP.

Best wishes

- 海关收税恶意纠纷（提供海关收据）。

思路：针对快递只要你提前与买家协商好渠道，申报价值，要付关税是买家自己的义务。

Dear Valued Friend,

Really sorry for that inconvenience. In fact, we sent you by DHL as you chose in my store, and before shipping, we have talked with you about the value, each we declare $*** on the package as we talked, and you need pay the tax for your customs. It is your obligation.

Or you can send the tax picture, we need check it first, and help you solve the problem ASAP.

Best wishes

Mission Implementation（任务实施）

学习了上述规则之后，Peter 和 Anne 开始着手自己的工作，即登录店铺后台管理平台，处理站内客户来信。图 5-15 所示为站内信处理页面。

图 5-15　卖家站内信处理页面

Task 1　Common After-sale Problems（常见售后问题）

Activity 1　Match the corresponding e-mail subject to the e-mail content（根据邮件内容匹配对应邮件主题）.

1）物流问题。

2）海关通关。

3）求好评。

4）退换货问题。

A. We were informed the package did not arrive due to shipping problems with the delivery company.

B. If you are not satisfied with the products, you can return the goods back to us.

C. Because the Spain and Haly Customs are much stricter than any other European countries, the parcels to these two countries often meet "Customs Inspection."

D. Your shopping experience is very important to us and our business. We would like to invite you to leave positive feedback on our products and services.

Task 2　Payment Delay（支付延迟）

客户下了单，却迟迟未付款。要了解客户未及时付款的原因，撰写售后催款邮件，掌握催款邮件应包含的重要内容。买家下单后不付款的原因有哪些呢？比如无法及时联系卖家对细节进行确认；发现运费过高；对同类商品需要再进行比较；付款过程出现问题；对卖家信誉产生疑虑等。

Activity 1　Peter sent an internal letter to the buyer, please match the subject to each section of the e-mail（客服 Peter 给买家发了一封站内信，请根据邮件各部分内容匹配对应主题）.

Dear friend,
1. We appreciated your purchase from us.

2. However, we notice that you haven't made the payment yet. This is a friendly reminder to you to complete the payment transaction as soon as possible.

3. Instant payments are very important; the earlier you pay, the sooner you will get the item.

4. If you have any problem making the payment, or if you don't want to go through with the order, please let us know. We can help you resolve the payment problem or cancel the order.

5. Thanks again! Looking forward to hearing from you soon.

Best Regards,

Peter

请根据邮件各部分内容匹配对应主题

A. Tell the importance of payment.

B. Thanks for the purchase.

C. Looking forward to a reply.

D. Point out the problem.

E. Ask questions.

Activity 2　Please analyze the effect of the letter from Anne（分析 Anne 发出的这封信的作用）．

Dear friend,

We appreciate your order from us. You have chosen one of the best selling products in our store.

It's very popular for its good quality and competitive price. Right now, we only have 5 pieces. We would like to inform you that this product has a high risk of selling out soon.

We noticed that you hadn't finished the payment process for the order. We'd like to offer you a 10% discount on your order, if you purchase now, to ensure that the product doesn't sell out. We will ship your order within 24 hours once your payment is confirmed.

If you need any help or have any question, please let us know.

Best regards,

Anne

1）这封信的作用是什么呢？为了买家能尽快付款，邮件提到：

A. Because of a shortage of inventory, remind the buyer of the payment as soon as possible.

B. Response to the buyers' bargaining.

C. Inform the buyers of the products out of stock.

2）为了使买家能尽快付款，邮件提到以下哪几点？

A. 产品价格优势。

B. 取消订单流程。

C. 折扣优惠。

D. 产品品质优势。

E. 库存不足。

F. 卖家信誉。

Activity 3　Practice for urging payment（售后催款范例练习）.

Dear friend,

　　We appreciate your purchase from us.

　　However, ___1___. This is a friendly reminder of you to complete the payment transaction as soon as possible. ___2___; the earlier you pay, the sooner you will get the item. ___3___ or if you don't want to go through with the order, ___4___. We can help you resolve the payment problem or cancel the order. Thanks again!

Best regards,

Peter

　　A. Looking forward to hearing from you soon

　　B. please let us know

　　C. we notice that you haven't made the payment yet

　　D. Instant payments are very important

　　E. If you have any problem in making the payment

Task 3　Customs Inspection（海关检察）

Dear friend,

1. 表示感谢。 2. 回复是否可以发往指定国家。 3. 告知运输途中遇到的问题。 4. 告知航行时间。 5. 礼貌结尾。

Sincerely,

　　A. As we know from our former experience, normally it will take 25 to 45 days to arrive at your country.

　　B. Because the Spain and Italy Customs are much stricter than any other European countries, the parcels to these two countries often meet "Customs Inspection." That makes the shipping time hard to control.

　　C. Yes, actually we can send these items to Italy. However, there' only one problem.

　　D. Please feel free to contact me. Waiting for your reply!

　　E. Thank you for your inquiry.

Task 4　Shipping Problems（装运问题）

Activity 1　The buyer has not received the goods due to shipping logistics and has been informed of the re-shipment（航运物流导致买家未收到货物，告知买家已重新发货）.

Dear friend,

　　Thank you for your inquiry. _____

Project 5　After-sale Service（售后客服）

However, we were informed the package did not arrive due to shipping problems with the delivery company.

We have re-sent your order by EMS; the new tracking number is: RR896762167CN.

We are very sorry for the inconvenience.

If you have any further question, please feel free to contact me.

Best regards,

Jessie

Thank you for your patience.

It usually takes 7 days to arrive at your destination.

We would like to confirm that we sent the package on 30 Feb, 2016.

I am happy to contact you.

Task 5　Feedback Requirement（反馈要求）

客服专员要尽量保证客户给予好的评价，尽量避免中差评的出现。客户给差评的原因主要有货物运送时间的合理性、实物商品与图片有差异、客服人员的沟通质量及回复速度等。那我们如何避免和解决差评呢？首先，做好完善的服务；其次，遇到问题时要有效及时地与客户沟通；再次，严格把关产品自身质量；最后，要做好中差评营销。

Activity 1　Read the message to determine the subject and find the right answer（请解读邮件内容，确定主题并找到正确匹配项）.

Dear friend,

---

1. Thank you for your shopping with us.

2. We are very happy you have received your parcel. Thank you again for your shopping in our store. We hope you are satisfied with our product and service.

3. If you feel good with everything, please kindly leave a positive 5 - star feedback to us.

4. If there is any problem, please feel free to tell us. Thank you very much and have a good day!

Sincerely,

Annie

　　A. 表示感谢。

　　B. 礼貌结尾。

　　C. 确认已收货。

　　D. 追好评。

Activity 2　After receiving the product, the buyer is not very satisfied with the product. It may need to return or replace the product. Put the following sentences in the right place（买家收到产品后，对产品不是很满意，可能需要退换货。将下面句子恰当排序填在合适的位置）.

> Dear friend,
>
> _____
> _____
> _____
>
> We hope to do business with you for a long time.
> _____
>
> Best regards,
> Annie

When we receive the goods, we will give you a replacement or give you a full refund.

If you are not satisfied with the products, you can return the goods back to us.

We will give you a big discount in your next order.

I'm sorry for the inconvenience.

Activity 3　Understand the message to determine the subject（理解邮件内容以确定主题）.

> Dear friend,
> We feel very sorry that you are unsatisfied with our product or service.
> Please contact us at any time to tell us the problem when you are available. We will do our best to resolve your problem. We hope you can revise your negative feedback into a 4 - or 5 - star positive
> feedback. Sorry for any inconvenience. If there is any problem, please feel free to tell us.
> Thank you very much.
> Yours sincerely,
> Peter

　　A. 收到差评，希望修改评价。
　　B. 提醒买家收货后给予好评。
　　C. 收到好评给予答谢。

Case Study-Handling disputes of platform stores（案例分析——平台店铺纠纷处理）

　　客户与店铺如果发生纠纷，客服专员该如何处理呢？首先应搞清楚客户的收货状况，是货物被海关扣押、货物破损、货物与描述不符、货物存在质量问题、销售了假货、物流显示妥投客户却说没收到货，还是查无物流信息等。通常，有两种情况：一是客户未收到货；二是货不对版。根据平台对店铺不同的考核点和处罚措施，匹配对应的平台纠纷处罚。纠纷提起率是卖家被提起纠纷的情况，会影响卖家的产品曝光；货不对版裁决提起率是卖家未解决的货不对版纠纷提交至平台裁决的情况，货不对版卖家责任裁决率是速卖通平台裁决的货不对版卖家责任纠纷订单的情况，后两者不仅会影响卖家的产品曝光，比率过高会导致产品一段时间内无法被买家搜索到。

平台对纠纷的考核关键 KPI 指标如下：

1. 纠纷提起率：一定周期内买家提起退款的订单数与发货订单数之比。
2. 裁决提起率：一定周期内提交至平台进行裁决的订单数与发货订单数之比。
3. 卖家责任裁决率：一定周期内提交至平台进行裁决并且最终被判为卖家的责任的订单数与发货订单数之比。

> 纠纷处罚指标数据计算方法：
> 纠纷提起率 = 周期内（买家提起退款的订单数 - 买家主动撤销退款的订单数）÷ 周期内（买家确认收货 + 确认收货超时 + 买家提起退款）的订单数

> 裁决提起率 = 提交至速卖通平台进行裁决的纠纷订单数 ÷ 周期内（买家确认收货 + 确认收货超时 + 买家提起退款并解决 + 提交至速卖通平台进行裁决）的订单数

> 卖家责任裁决率 = 提交至速卖通平台进行裁决且最终被裁定为卖家责任的纠纷订单数 ÷ 周期内（买家确认收货 + 确认收货超时 + 买家提起退款并解决 + 提交至速卖通平台进行裁决并裁决结束）的订单数

Activity 1　According to the buyer's dispute initiation, calculate the shop dispute punishment index（根据买家的纠纷提起情况，计算店铺纠纷处罚指标）.

售后客服专员 Annie 统计出童装店铺一段时间内的纠纷数据如下：买家确认收货共 20 笔，其中确认收货超时 3 笔，买家要求退款 5 笔，经客服沟通，其中买家取消退款申请并确认收货 1 笔，已与买家协商解决的有 2 笔，协商未成提交至平台方进行裁决的有 2 笔，平台裁定为卖家责任的 1 笔，还未裁决的订单 1 笔，请帮她计算出这段时间内该童装店铺的纠纷提起率、裁决提起率、卖家责任裁决率三项关键的平台对店铺的考核 KPI 指标（保留 2 位小数）。

Activity 2　Please judge what mistakes have been made in the store's product display according to the following product listing（请根据如图 5-16 所示产品详情页展示的内容判断该店铺产品展示出现了什么错误）.

图 5-16　产品详情页（一）

A. 颜色描述有误。

B. 销售单位有误。

C. 图片与标题描述不符。

Activity 3　Please judge what mistakes have been made in the store's product display according to the following product listing（请根据如图 5 – 17 所示产品详情页展示的内容判断该店铺产品展示出现了什么错误）.

图 5 – 17　产品详情页（二）

Cross-border E-commerce English-Chinese Vocabulary（跨境电商英汉术语对照）

1.	customs liquidation		清关
2.	inevitable	adj.	不可避免的
3.	accept	v.	接受
4.	after-sale service		售后服务
5.	arbitration	n.	仲裁
6.	cancel	v.	取消
7.	charge/fee	n.	（收）费
8.	claim	v.	索赔
9.	claimant	n.	提赔方（人）
10.	commodity inspection		商品检验
11.	complaint	n.	投诉
12.	compromise	n.	折中，妥协
13.	condemned goods		有问题的货物
14.	consignee	n.	收货人
15.	consignor	n.	发货人
16.	contract	n.	合同
17.	coupon	n.	优惠券
18.	customs	n.	海关
19.	customer	n.	客户
20.	customer satisfaction		客户满意度

21.	customs clearance		结关
22.	customs inspection		海关在验
23.	customs duty		关税
24.	damage	v.	损坏
25.	dead freight		空舱费
26.	defective	adj.	有缺陷的；不完美的
27.	delivery	n.	交货
28.	discount coupon		优惠券
29.	dispute	n.	争议
30.	eta：estimated (expected) time of arrival		预计到达时间
31.	evidence	n.	证据
32.	exchange	n.	换货
33.	expire	v.	期满
34.	feedback	n.	反馈
35.	file a complaint		投诉
36.	guarantee	v.	保证
37.	logistic information		物流信息
38.	look into		调查
39.	mediation	n.	调解
40.	mediation of dispute		争议调解
41.	negative	adj.	负面的，消极的
42.	negotiation	n.	协商
43.	neutral	adj.	中立的
44.	ocean/sea freight		海运费
45.	package	n.	包裹
46.	positive	adj.	正面的，积极的
47.	proceed	v.	进行
48.	proposal	n.	提议
49.	refund	v.	退款
50.	replacement	n.	更换
51.	resolve	v.	解决
52.	response time		响应时间
53.	return	v.	退货
54.	sales confirmation		销售确认书
55.	solution	n.	解决方案
56.	stock	n.	存货，库存量
57.	surcharge/additional charge		额外费用
58.	the shipper party		托运方
59.	track	v.	追踪

60. transaction		n.	交易
61. transit		n.	运输
62. upload		v.	上传
63. within time limit			在规定期限内

Project 6

Sales Promotion（促销活动）

Learning Aims（学习目标）

From learning this chapter, students can plan various holiday sales and write sales promotion e-mails to customers on cross-border e-commerce platform, interacting with customers to promote sales.

1. Understand the culture background of major festivals in West to prepare for holiday sales.
2. Exercise the ability to write sales promotion e-mails for different subjects.
3. Learn to promote your shop and participate in platform activities.
4. Grasp the characteristics of English advertisement and learn to publish advertisements in a commercial way.

Lead-in Situation（项目背景）

麋鹿服装贸易公司以销售青年男女休闲服装为主。该公司的产品主打各类牛仔单品，同时也销售搭配牛仔服饰的 T 恤衫、休闲外套等。客服的 Tim 最近正在规划下一季度的各类营销活动。他发现虽然店铺近期销售量比较稳定，但是在客户营销方面还有很多应当改进的地方。他决定做一个系统的规划，希望通过未来有效的客户营销能够进一步促进公司产品销量，提高客户满意度与忠诚度。

Cross-border E-commerce Platform Sales Promotion Classification（跨境电商平台促销活动分类）

一、Festivals and Holidays Marketing（重要节庆日客户营销）

企业可以利用西方的各类节庆日进行节假日促销，主要是在节日期间通过各种优惠活动吸引客户。作为跨境电商从业人员，必须掌握和了解西方主要节庆日以及相关的风俗，有针对性地开展促销活动，吸引客户到店内下单购买。

二、New Arrivals Marketing（新产品上市客户营销）

在企业新产品上市时进行专门的新品推介活动。新品上市能否被顾客接受和喜爱要通过市场的检验，有效的营销活动能够吸引到更多新客户，同时提升老客户的忠诚度，促进新产品的销售。

三、Regular Customers Marketing（老客户回馈营销）

企业可以通过店庆周年活动、老客户积分兑换活动等向老客户发送促销活动邮件，吸引老客户到店下单购物，从而不断培养客户的忠诚度，提升企业的品牌价值。

四、Store Promotion and Platform Promotion（店铺日常推广与平台活动）

通过对产品和店铺进行推广，及时参加跨境电商平台的各项活动，吸引新老客户到店，从而增加转化率是很重要的客户营销途径。店铺推广主要是店主根据自己的商品选择适合的营销方式向顾客推送商品。平台活动是各个交易平台面向卖家推出的免费推广服务，一般来讲店铺参与平台活动应当符合平台有关的要求。在店铺日常推广与平台活动中，要经常使用广告英语，因此要掌握广告英语的表达技巧。

Green-hand Guide（新手指南）

一、Key Points of Festivals and Holidays Marketing（节庆日客户营销要点）

1. 西方国家的大型节庆日有新年、情人节、愚人节、母亲节、父亲节、万圣节、感恩节、圣诞节、复活节。西方人在不同的节庆日有不同的采购习惯，也传递不一样的情感。卖家可以详细了解每一个节日的意义、习俗、消费者所采购的用品等，结合公司产品进行营销活动。

（1）元旦/新年（1月1日）。

新年（New Year）为纪念1582年罗马教皇格列高利十三世而采用此历命名。按阳历或公历，新年从1月1日开始。在西方元旦这一天，人们辞旧迎新，有多种庆祝活动。西方一般在圣诞节与新年会连续放假休息，这也是各商家全年销售的黄金时间周（图6-1）。

6-1 平台活动　　6-2 店铺营销

图6-1　西方节日示例（1）

（2）情人节（2月14日）。

情人节（Valentine's Day）又称"瓦伦丁节"。这一习俗远溯到古罗马的"牧神节"。为纪念畜牧之神卢泊库斯的功绩，每逢这一天人们总要举行各种舞会和游戏。特别是在抽签游戏中，每个男青年可以从"签筒"中抽出写有某少女名字的签，被抽中的姑娘便成了他的情人。这种有趣的节日游戏，后来渐渐取代了"牧神节"的意义，而成了青年恋人的节日，并由此传到了英、法等西欧各国。在英国，瓦伦丁节习俗的一个重要特征则是在这天你看见的第一位异性成为你的情人。传到美国,经过几个世纪的演变,它已完全成为人们互相交流感情的节日。在这一天人们制作、购买精美的工艺美术品,如鲜花、巧克力、饰品、画片、明信片等礼物,内藏甜言蜜语,用以交流情感。因此它是一个爱情的节日、友谊的节日、欢乐的节日(图6-2)。

图6-2 西方节日示例(2)

(3) 愚人节(4月1日)。

每年4月1日是西方的愚人节(April Fool's Day)。在这天中午12点以前,人们可以尽情地互相捉弄和欺骗。受骗者被人戏称为"傻瓜""笨蛋"(fool)!对此,人们不但不以为然,反而感到高兴。这一习俗起源于英国,后来由于其独特的情趣,逐渐传至西欧各地,并受到人们的喜爱。在愚人节里,不仅男女老幼之间互相愚弄、谎骗而取乐,就连电视、电台和报纸偶尔也会精心设计"假报道"来骗观众、听众和读者(图6-3)。

图6-3 西方节日示例(3)

(4) 母亲节(5月的第二个星期日)。

每年五月的第二个星期日为母亲节(Mother's Day)。1906年5月9日,美国费城一位名叫安娜·查维斯女子的慈母去世了,她的母亲原是一位教员。第二年,当查维斯在教堂中举行纪念祈祷会时,提议全国在每年定出一天来表示对所有母亲的纪念和尊敬。她说:"她们受苦最多,所得到的报答最少。平时我们想不到尊敬她,直到她离去后才省悟。"1913年5月10日美国国会通过一项法令,决定每年五月第二个星期日为"母亲节"。后传到西方各国。在这一天,人们到教堂去做礼拜,为各自的母亲祝福,为母亲献上一张节日卡片或小礼物,或请他们的母亲去饭馆就餐(图6-4)。

图6-4 西方节日示例(4)

(5)父亲节(6月的第三个星期日)。

世界上的第一个父亲节(Father's Day)于1910年诞生在美国,是由住在美国华盛顿州斯波坎(Spokane)的布鲁斯多德夫人(Mrs. Dodd,Sonora Louise Smart Dodd)倡导的。她年幼丧母,兄弟姐妹六人全靠父亲抚养成人。父亲的这种既为人父又为人母的自我牺牲精神极大地感动了她。长大后,她积极倡导父亲节,后来在1916年她的建议得到了Woodwork Wilson总统的官方承认。从此父亲节便成了美国的一项传统节日。世界上有52个国家和地区是在每年6月的第三个星期日庆祝父亲节的。节日里有各种庆祝方式,大部分都与赠送礼物、家族聚餐或活动有关(图6-5)。

图6-5 西方节日示例(5)

(6)万圣节(10月31日)。

万圣节也称鬼节(Halloween)。在这个节日里小孩们装扮成"鬼"去敲每家每户的门,嘴里喊着"Trick or Treat",于是他们得到糖果、礼品等,可谓满载而归。几乎所有的男女青年都去参加夜间举行的化装游行或舞会。他们都把自己打扮成魔鬼、动物、古代人、外星人、机器人等奇形怪状的样子,表演各种各样的令人难以置信的动作,发出刺耳的声音,呈现出一幕幕离奇、荒唐的场景。很多地区每年都会组织举行大型化装游行活动,热闹非凡。节日象征物为:内点蜡烛、镂刻各式鬼脸的"南瓜灯"(图6-6)。

图 6-6 西方节日示例（6）

（7）感恩节（11 月第 4 个星期四）。

感恩节（Thanksgiving）是北美及西欧各地的传统节日。节日期间为每年 11 月第四个星期的星期四至星期天，为四天假期。感恩节始于 1621 年，已有 390 多年历史。它源于一个动人的历史故事。1620 年 9 月，有 102 名英国清教徒乘"五月花号"木船，经过 65 天的海上漂泊，于 11 月 21 日抵达美国东北部的普洛维登斯附近的普利茅斯，找到了一个印第安人村落。当地印第安人很同情这些移民，帮助他们狩猎、捕鱼、种庄稼，并取得了丰收。移民们感谢上帝的赐予和印第安人的帮助，于 1621 年秋天用火鸡、南瓜、玉米、红薯等劳动果实大摆宴席。当时还有近百名印第安人带着火鸡、鹿等礼品应邀前来赴宴，一连庆祝三天三夜，如此年复一年。节日象征物及必备食品为"火鸡"（turkey）（图 6-7）。

图 6-7 西方节日示例（7）

（8）圣诞节（12 月 25 日）。

圣诞节是欧美国家一年中最重要的节日。它原本是耶稣基督诞辰纪念日，如今已成为西方国家全民性的节日，颇似中国的春节。圣诞节定于每年 12 月 25 日，节日期间一般为 12 月 24 日到翌年 1 月 6 日。这段时期里，雪片般的贺卡飞往世界各地，电话线、通信网频繁地传递人们的祝福和问候；大街小巷粉饰一新，商店橱窗前大减价、大拍卖的广告格外醒目；到处可见人们拎着大包小包的节日用品匆匆而过，到处可听见欢快的歌声和笑声。车站、机场里此时挤满了盼望回家的人群，因为圣诞节也是家人团聚的日子。无论外出多远，人们都会想方设法赶回家与亲人团聚。圣诞节期间，夫妻之间、亲友间都将互赠节日礼品

(Christmas gift)。节日的象征物为圣诞树（小松树）、圣诞花、圣诞蜡烛、圣诞卡、圣诞邮票、圣诞老人、鹿（reindeer）、拐杖形糖（sugar cane）（图6-8）。

图6-8 西方节日示例（8）

（9）复活节（春分前后）。

复活节（Easter Day）是一个西方的重要节日，在每年春分月圆之后第一个星期日。基督教徒认为，复活节象征着重生与希望，为纪念耶稣基督于公元30—33年被钉死在十字架之后第三天复活的日子。其日期是不固定的，通常是要查看日历才能知道。大多数家庭会有聚餐活动。复活节彩蛋精美漂亮且富有装饰性，它们代表着人们的美好心愿，人们可以借以分享季节更替的喜悦。复活节的另一象征是小兔子，原因是它具有极强的繁殖能力，人们视它为新生命的创造者（图6-9）。

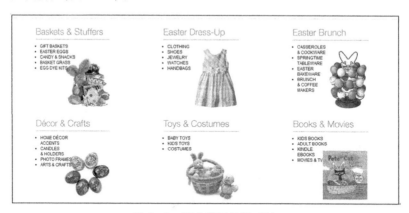

图6-9 西方节日示例（9）

2. 在节庆日期间，邮件营销的撰写应当特别注重邮件标题与邮件内容。

（1）邮件标题可以尝试换一些醒目的色彩，标题应该有公司的信息。

（2）邮件正文应当说明是什么样的节假日、有哪些优惠活动、店铺的网址等。

（3）结尾可以附上与节日信息相关的主题活动。

二、New Arrivals Marketing（新产品上市客户营销）

在店铺推出新品时，可以用醒目的新品上市标语作为邮件的主题，同时店铺网址首页也应当及时更新，在邮件中运用有感召力的话语提示客户关注新品，写明店铺针对购买新品的顾客提供的折扣或附加优惠。图 6-10 所示为速卖通某女装店铺新品上市活动截图。

图 6-10　新品上市活动截图

三、Regular Customers Marketing（老客户回馈营销）

老客户回馈一般指为在店铺内有一次及以上购买经历的客户提供的购买优惠，它是很重要的一种客户营销思路。店铺一般选择在店庆日、店铺重大活动或其他节庆日回馈老客户，一般会为老客户提供优惠券、满额赠礼品、限时领取老客户专属纪念品、消费积分兑换等不同类型的优惠活动。

> Notes:
> 周年店庆活动 Anniversary Sale
> 您将享受全场 4 折优惠 You will enjoy 60% off for the entire shop.
> 低至五折 Up to 50% off
> 请联系我们 Please feel free to contact us

四、Store Promotion and Platform Promotion（店铺日常推广与平台活动）

（一）店铺日常推广

1. 店铺首页推广。

店铺的首页是一个店铺的招牌和门面，当客户浏览到店铺时，精美的主图或具有视觉冲击力的画面能够吸引客户停留在该店铺并进入相关商品详情页面仔细查看。买家在店铺内停留时间越长，那么客户的购买欲望也越强烈。在店铺首页推广中，注意把握以下原则：

（1）店铺首页有明确的色彩视觉表现，店铺基调风格一致，使访问店铺的客户第一时间明确商品定位与销售对象。

（2）应当在店铺的最佳展示位置，也就是前三屏放置店铺主打商品，并做好单个商品详情页面优化。

（3）店铺分类栏目要便捷，帮助买家快速找到自己感兴趣的商品。

图 6-11 所示为速卖通某女装店铺首页推广的前三屏。

(a)

(b)

(c)

图 6-11　速卖通某女装店铺首页推广的前三屏

2. 橱窗推广。

橱窗是网店平台给不同信誉等级的店铺相应的优先展示位，相当于商店门口玻璃橱窗的位置，可以起到让没有进到店铺的消费者都能看到店铺里的某些商品的优先展示作用，商品搜索时会优先排列有推荐橱窗的商品。不同的平台橱窗位赠送的数量与规则都不尽相同。速卖通平台上，商家上传商品超过 120 件即多送一个橱窗位。图 6-12 所示为速卖通男装橱窗展示情况。

图6-12　速卖通男装橱窗展示情况

3. 关联推广。

关联推广是在一个商品页面同时放置其他同类、同品牌可搭配的有关联的商品，实现深层次的多面引导。主要有三种关联方法：

（1）互补型关联推广：强调搭配的商品和主推商品有直接相关性，例如主推商品为泳装，可以搭配泳镜、泳帽等（图6-13）。

（2）替代关联推广：指主推商品和关联商品可以完全替代，例如圆领T恤，关联为V领T恤等。

（3）潜在关联推广：重点强调潜在互补关系，特别对多类目店铺可以考虑这种方法。例如户外用品与聚会用品，表面上两种产品关联不强，但是潜在意义上，去户外的人可能在户外有聚会活动。

图6-13　速卖通关联推广示例

（二）平台活动

平台活动通常为在特定行业、特定主题下的产品推广活动。每一期活动都会在相应平台的"营销中心"频道中进行招商。商家可以用符合招商条件的产品报名参选，一旦入选，其产品就会出现在活动的发布页面，获得推广。使用平台活动可以曝光商品，获得流量，提高转化率。但是平台活动一般设置的门槛较高，获得参与平台活动的机会相对较少。

以速卖通平台为例，了解平台活动的类别与技巧：

（1）平台活动类别：常规活动指平台日常举办的主题活动，速卖通平台有俄罗斯团购、巴西团购等；行业主题活动指针对诸如童装、母婴产品的专题平台活动；平台大促是指不同的平台每年会不定期举办平台大型促销活动；品牌馆活动指平台的一些知名品牌有时会和平台联合举行一些品牌馆活动。参与品牌馆活动，首先要符合平台要求的规则，比如品牌要求、产品质量证明等。

（2）参与平台活动需要注意的事项：注意时间问题，应每天查看活动更新，平台一般会在下午 5—6 点更新活动；参加平台活动时要注意报名的产品与招商的目的一致，否则会造成错误乃至浪费。例如，参加巴西团购平台活动，参加之后才发现自己的产品运费模板无法到达巴西；参加平台活动如果适当体现一些价格优势会使平台活动效果发挥得更好；参与平台活动一定要将报名产品的信息填写完整。

（3）平台活动技巧总结：确定活动对产品和店铺的要求，严格按照活动要求参加活动；商品要应季，重视客户评价；在速卖通平台的俄罗斯团购和巴西团购中如果商家免邮，那么被选上的概率就很大。要有历史销量数据，商品详情页页面要整洁、尺寸要清晰。

图 6-14 所示为速卖通俄罗斯团购活动。

图 6-14　速卖通平台活动示例

（三）广告英语特点

在店铺或平台活动中推送英文广告，要把握广告英语的特点。广告英语有以下特点：

1）广告英语的词汇特点。

（1）简明易懂，通俗易记。

广告文字必须具备通俗易懂的特性，多用大众化的口语词汇，使消费者看得明白、说得清楚。

Nike, just do it. （耐克，想做就做。）

Scots Whisky Uncommonly Smooth. （苏格兰威士忌口感滋润非同凡响。）

（2）创新拼写，增强吸引力。

在广告英语中，创作人员会故意把人们所熟知的词拼错，或加上前缀、后缀。虽然新造词与原词形态不同，但意义仍存，这既可以达到生动、有趣和引人注意的目的，又可以有效地传播商品信息。同时，人们往往认为用词富于创新的广告，其宣传的产品常具独特之处。

Give a Timex to all, to all a good Time. （拥有一块天美时表，拥有一段美好时光。）Timex = Time

For twogether the ultimate all inclusive one price sun kissed holiday. （两人共度一个阳光灿烂的假日，一切费用均包括在单人价格之内。）twogether 取自 together 之音，又取"两人"之意，比 together 更形象，倍添情趣。

（3）针对性强。

广告的目的就是让消费者尽可能多地了解产品。因此，创作者要抓住产品的主要特点，有的放矢，用形象、生动的语言表达，使消费者在不经意间记住产品。

Tide's in, Dirt's out。（汰渍放进去，污垢洗出来。——汰渍洗衣粉）这是一则针对性很强的洗衣粉广告，消费者自然心领神会。

2）广告英语的句法特点。

（1）多用简单句。

广告是面向全体消费者的，这就要求语言简练、简单，即在语言结构上要多用简单句，少用复杂句，让消费者看得懂、记得住。

We're not in the computer business. We're in me results business. （唯我电脑，成效更高。——电脑）

（2）多用祈使句和疑问句。

在广告英语中用祈使句和疑问句，其目的是敦促消费者积极作出反应、采取行动。

Buy one pair, get one free. （买一，送一。）

Catch that Pepsi spirit, drink it in. （喝百事饮料，振百事精神。）

3）广告英语的修辞特点。

修辞是使语言表达准确、生动的一种文字运用手法，也是使文字表达的内容给人以深刻印象的有效手段。修辞用得好，能起到事半功倍的效果。从某种程度上说，借助修辞，可以提高广告的感染力，达到打动消费者的目的。

（1）排比。

排比修辞手法运用于广告中，可以从文字上增强语势，从而加深消费者的印象。

No problem too large. No business too small. （没有解决不了的大问题，没有不做的小生意——IBM 广告）

（2）拟人。

广告文字的拟人化，可以使所宣传的产品人格化，赋予产品以生命。

Unlike me, my Rolex never needs a rest. （和我不一样，我的劳力克斯从不需要休息——手表广告）

（3）押韵。

押韵可使广告富有节奏感，读起来朗朗上口，听起来赏心悦耳。

Hi-fi, Hi-fun, Hi-fashion, only for Sony. （高保真，高乐趣，高时尚——索尼）

（4）反复。

反复是通过重复某一词或词组使人加深印象，给人强烈刺激，增强广告效果。

Extra Taste, Not Extra Calories. （额外的口味，并无额外的热量——食品广告）

（5）明喻。

Featherwater: light as a feather. （法泽瓦特眼镜：轻如鸿毛。）

（6）双关。

Ask for More. （摩尔牌香烟的广告）

（7）借用谚语。

Where there is a way for car, there is a Toyota. （车到山前必有路，有路必有丰田车。）

（8）重复。

Dish after dish after dish. People expect us to be better. （一盘一盘又一盘，人们希望我们会更好。）

Mission Implementation（任务实施）

学习了客户营销有关知识后，Tim 开始着手自己的工作，在新年的第一季度，即将迎来情人节，他决定进行一次节假日促销。

Task 1　Holiday Promotion（节假日促销）

Activity 1　Making plan of festivals and holidays marketing（制定节假日促销方案）.

1）双重优惠。

2）五到八折。

3）订单满 19 美元减 2 美元，满 39 美元减 5 美元，满 49 美元减 7 美元。

4）活动主题：想要独一无二的情人节？

请为促销方案匹配正确的英文表达方式：

A. 20% off to 50% off.

B. Want a different and indelible Valentine's Day?

C. Get $2 off on orders of $19, get $5 off on orders of $39, get $7 off on orders of $49.

D. get double discount.

Activity 2　Writing e-mails of festivals and holidays marketing（撰写节假日促销邮件）.

距离即将到来的情人节（图 6-15）还有一个多月时间，Tim 准备在速卖通平台向全体老客户群发活动通知邮件，进行邮件营销。在撰写邮件之前，主管 Bill 对他提了几点注意事项：

1）撰写邮件标题的注意事项：

（1）公司名称应体现在邮件标题中。

（2）关键词可以用不同颜色或字体标出。

（3）不要总是使用同一个主题。

（4）不要在邮件标题上标注姓名。

（5）想象自己是一位顾客，发送邮件前可以进行几次测试。

2）撰写邮件正文的注意事项：

（1）正文应匹配主题活动的图片以增强客户阅读效果。

（2）将公司的 LOGO（图 6-16）在发送营销邮件的时候总是放在同一个位置。

（3）用词要简洁但不简单。

（4）使用统一的字体。

(5) 关键促销信息要用不同颜色的字体。

(6) 巧妙使用空行。

(7) 不要在图片中加入邮件正文内容。

图 6-15　速卖通情人节活动

图 6-16　麋鹿品牌标识

SUBJECT: Big Valentine's Day Promotion from ELK

Dear Customer,

Valentine's Day is coming soon. Are you ready for her/him?

We are preparing a big promotion from January 20th for your romantic Valentine's Day!

Visit our store: EIK! You can enjoy 20% off to 50% off or the entire shop from January 20th to January 22th.

Meanwhile you can get double discount: get \$2 off on orders of \$19, get \$5 off on orders of \$39, get \$7 off on orders of \$49, etc.

Please kindly visit our store and check if there is anything interesting for you.

Our website:

https://www.aliexpress.com/store/912070? spm = 2114.10010108.100005.2.335286d8TYG-5OO

Thank you very much for your shopping. Have a good time!

Tim

ELK Jeans Store

Task 2　Introducing New Arrivals（新品推介）

麋鹿牛仔服饰将于下一季度推出新的系列牛仔单品，Tim 需要向老客户们发邮件介绍新一季单品,并说明提前预订可享受相关优惠活动。于是,他开始着手准备新品推介的促销方案。

Activity 1　Making plan of new arrivals marketing(制定新品推介促销方案).

1)新款到店。

2)时尚牛仔。

3)限量水壶。

4)人数限定在……

5)请查看店内新款。

6)最新发布的产品。

请为促销方案匹配正确的英文表达方式:

A. See what's new in stores.

B. Fashion jeans.

C. Limit the number of customers to…

D. Limited edition sports kettle.

E. New arrivals.

F. Newest releases.

Activity 2　Writing e-mails of new arrivals marketing(撰写新品推介邮件).

根据之前主管 Bill 提醒他的注意事项,Tim 撰写了以下新品推介(图 6-17)促销邮件发给店内的所有老客户。请在下列词汇或短语中,选择相应内容填写到 Tim 的邮件空白处。

1. free
2. fashion jeans
3. with
4. waiting
5. order

图 6-17　麋鹿品牌新品推介活动

SUBJECT: NEW ARRIVALS! We're checking new out

Dear all,

Hot summer is coming. Start the new season ＿＿＿＿ this summer ＿＿＿＿!

Get our newest releases. If you _____ any new item, you will enjoy 25% off for new arrivals. Besides, you will also get a _____ limited edition sports kettle (only for top 100 customers). The sale will end on May 20. Come on, we are here _____ for you! See what's new in stores.
Tim
ELK Jeans Store

Task 3 Rewards for Old Customers（回馈老顾客）

麋鹿牛仔服饰将迎来三周年店庆，准备开展周年店庆活动。Tim 制定了 3 周年店庆回馈老客户活动条款，并撰写了相关促销邮件发送给了老客户。

Activity 1 Making plan of regular customers marketing（回馈老客户促销活动方案）.

1）周年店庆活动。
2）您将享受全场 4 折优惠。
3）当您购物满 $50 赠送神秘礼品。
4）优惠券。
5）请联系我们。
6）有效期。

请为促销方案匹配正确的英文表达方式：

A. Coupon.

B. Anniversary Sale.

C. Deals expire.

D. Have an extra mysterious gift when you spend $50 or more.

E. Please feel free to contact us.

F. You will enjoy 60% off for the entire shop.

Activity 2 Writing e-mails of regular customers marketing（撰写回馈老客户邮件）.

Tim 非常清楚这次三周年店庆活动（图 6 – 18）对公司十分重要，为此他专门请市场部的同事拍摄了符合店庆主题的海报并列好了营销邮件的提纲。

请按照提纲与上面的活动方案，补齐短缺的句子。

1. 说明三周年店庆活动时间。
2. 老客户在此期间享受全场四折优惠以及满 $50 神秘礼品赠送。
3. 在每名老顾客邮箱中赠送 $5 优惠券，可在规定日期前使用。
4. 可随时联系店铺了解活动有关细节。
5. 礼貌结尾。

图6-18 麋鹿品牌三周年店庆活动

SUBJECT: ANNIVERSARY SALE
Dear all,
Our 3 Anniversary Sale starts now from July 6 to July 8. You will enjoy _____, and an extra _____ when you _____. To extend our appreciation to you, _____. You can apply the coupon to your future order (Deals expire on July 6).
If you have any other concerns, _____. Have a good time!
Tim
ELK Jeans Store

Task 4　Advertising Items on the Home Page（首页推广活动）

随着越来越多西方人喜爱中国文化，中国农历新年也逐渐走入西方消费者视线。在中国农历狗年即将到来时，麋鹿牛仔服饰推出了中国农历新年款衬衫（图6-19）。Tim想在店铺首页进行推广。产品如下：

Activity 1　Product advertising slogan（产品广告语）.

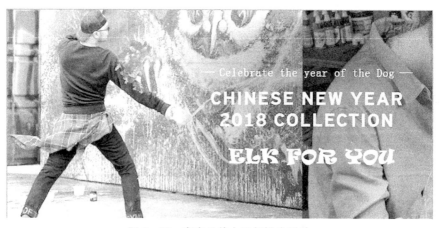

图6-19 麋鹿品牌中国年推广活动

Project 6 Sales Promotion（促销活动）

麋鹿服饰中国农历狗年纪念版衬衫在店铺首页上推送的英文广告为：
Lucky Dog is Coming! Being Lucky Dog in the new year!
Happy Chinese New Year!
幸运狗来啦！新的一年成为幸运儿！中国农历新年快乐！
点评：Lucky Dog 在英语中是习惯短语，意为幸运儿，在此与中国狗年相结合，有双关作用。

Activity2　Translate the following advertising slogan（翻译下列广告标语）.

1）网上周一 24 小时美裙大促销！仅限今日，千载难逢！
2）非凡性感系列前所未有的火热！米娅儿泳衣运动装！非凡性感系列让夏天更火热！
3）这个情人节给她惊喜——给她所爱。
4）新年计划很重要，但新年新祝福更重要！我们的冬季清仓活动将为您的新年派对增添更多色彩。赶紧来吧，就像那些精美的雪花，好东西转瞬即逝。
5）璀璨真我——大福珠宝，春季促销。

A. 24 – Hour Cyber Monday Sale! Great dresses! Today only! Don't miss out on these hot deals.

B. The very sexy collection is here and hotter than ever! Miyaer Bras Panties Swim Sport. Slip on a sexy little something and make summer even hotter!

C. Do Surprise her this Valentine's Day—with something she will love.

D. Resolutions are great, but celebration is better. Keep the party going with our absolute winter clearance sale. Hurry, like delicate snowflakes, the best picks won't last long.

E. The brilliance of each stone is the true inner. Dafu Jewelry, Spring Sales!

Task 5　Product Promotion（产品推广）

朵拉饰品在中国农历新年来临之际专门设计了十二生肖饰品，打算在速卖通平台的 Dora 饰品店铺进行新年店铺打折活动。打折力度为 20% ~ 50%，全场订单满 50 美元赠送首饰袋，订单满 100 美元立减 8 美元（图 6 – 20）。

Activity 1　Please send the e-mail to all the regular customers according to the above program（请根据上述节庆日客户营销方案，向全体老客户群发邮件，进行邮件营销）.

图 6 – 20　朵拉饰品中国年促销活动

朵拉饰品在中国农历新年促销活动中取得了不错的成绩，客服整理了近期的客户评价，商家可以通过这些评价总结经验，分析客户的需求，掌握客户在跨境电商中的消费心理。请帮助客服朵朵完成以下工作任务——根据中文内容填空：

Activity 2　Fill in the blanks according to the Chinese contents（根据中文内容填空）.

您的满意与好评对我们非常重要。如果您对我们的产品和服务感到满意，请留下您的好评和五星评价。如果您对产品和服务不满意，请在给出差评前先与我们联系。我们将尽力解决任何问题，提供给您最好的客户服务。

Your _____ and _____ feedback is very important to us. Please leave _____ feedback and _____ if you are satisfied with our _____.

If you have any problem with our _____, please feel free to contact us first before you leave _____ feedback. We will do our best to solve any problem and provide you with the best customer service.

Cross-border E-commerce English-Chinese Vocabulary（跨境电商英汉术语对照）

1. marketing　　　　　　　　　　　*n.*　　　　　营销
2. subject　　　　　　　　　　　　*n. & adj.*　　标题，主题；服从的
3. sales promotion　　　　　　　　　　　　　　产品促销
4. flash sale　　　　　　　　　　　　　　　　　限时折扣
5. anniversary sale　　　　　　　　　　　　　　周年店庆
6. free shipping　　　　　　　　　　　　　　　包邮
7. new arrivals　　　　　　　　　　　　　　　　新品
8. rewards for customers　　　　　　　　　　　回馈客户
9. coupon　　　　　　　　　　　　*n.*　　　　　优惠券
10. deals expire　　　　　　　　　　　　　　　有效期
11. customers' feedback　　　　　　　　　　　客户评价
12. good feedback　　　　　　　　　　　　　　好评
13. bad feedback　　　　　　　　　　　　　　　差评
14. Social Networking Services　　　　　　　　社交媒体网络服务平台（SNS）
15. festival　　　　　　　　　　　　*n.*　　　　节日，庆祝

Project 7

SNS Marketing (社交媒体推广)

Learning Aims (学习目标)

From learning this chapter, students can get knowledge of main popular social medias, master proper marketing methods of SNS platform, and can use it to market for cross-border el-commerce platform.

1. Understand the concept of SNS.
2. Get knowledge of main SNS platform.
3. Grasp marketing methods of Facebook and try to make an advertisement on Facebook.

Lead-in Situation (项目背景)

小王子公司在亚马逊平台上开了一家儿童玩具店,专营儿童玩具。店铺开张一段时间了,但是销量平平。老板希望通过社交媒体提升跨境电商店铺的流量,于是派客服部的职员Marry 和 Steve 专门负责该店铺的社交媒体推广工作。希望他们能够在深入调查网络社交媒体的基础上,制定详细的社交媒体推广方案。要想做好社交媒体推广,首先要了解国际上主流的社交媒体平台及每个平台的特色。

社交网站的概念及主流社交平台介绍如下。

一、SNS Introduction (社交网站介绍)

SNS 全称为 Social Networking Services (社交媒体网络服务平台),专指帮助人们建立社会性网络的互联网应用服务。SNS 的另一种解释是:Social Network Site, 即 "社交网站"。社会性网络是指人与人之间的关系网络,这种基于社会网络关系系统思想所建立的网站就是社交网站。国际上主流的社交媒体网络服务平台包括:Facebook、Twitter、Instagram、Pinterest、VK 等。

二、Major Social Media Platforms (主要社交媒体网络服务平台)

(一) Facebook

Facebook (脸书) 是美国的一个社交网络服务网站,创立于 2004 年 2 月 4 日,总部位于美国加利福尼亚州帕拉阿图,主要创始人为马克·扎克伯格。Facebook 是世界排名第一的照片分享站点,也是世界最大的社交网络平台。Facebook 的访问人群显示,来自美国的客户占比明显是最大的(图 7–1),其次是速卖通上的热销国家巴西。

图 7-1　Facebook 个人主页

(二) Twitter

Twitter（非官方汉语通称推特）是一家美国社交网络及微博客户服务网站。它可以让用户更新不超过 140 个字符的消息，这些消息也被称作"推文（Tweet）"。这个服务是由杰克·多西在 2006 年 3 月创办并在当年 7 月启动的。Twitter 在全世界都非常流行，据 Twitter 现任 CEO 迪克·科斯特洛宣布，截至 2017 年，Twitter 共有 3.28 亿个活跃用户，Twitter 被形容为"互联网的短信服务"（图 7-2）。

图 7-2　Twitter 页面

(三) Instagram

Instagram 这个名字源自 Instamatic，是柯达从 1963 年便开始销售的一个低价便携傻瓜相机的系列名。

它是一款运行在移动端上的 APP，优化拍摄、上传等细节，使得用户可以随时随地使用

Instagram;滤镜的处理,使得图片内容质量上升,以一种快速、美妙和有趣的方式将随时抓拍下的图片彼此分享(图7-3)。

图7-3 Instagram 示例

(四)Pinterest

Pinterest 采用的是瀑布流的形式展现图片内容,无须用户翻页,把自己感兴趣的东西用图钉钉在钉板(Pin Board)上。新的图片不断自动加载在页面底端,让用户不断地发现新的图片。用户女性居多,目前活跃用户约 8 000 万个。对于时尚女装、饰品等来说是不错的营销平台(图7-4)。

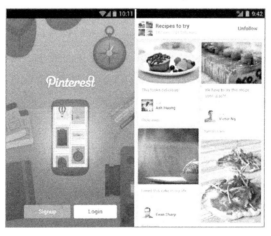

图7-4 Pinterest 示例

Green-hand Guide(新手指南)

一、Facebook Ads Overview(脸书广告概述)

Facebook 成立至今,活跃用户的个数已突破 20 亿大关,成为全球规模最大、最具影响力的社交媒体平台。面对如此巨大的市场,跨境电商商家纷纷在思考,如何能利用该平台为自己的网店引入流量。

在 Facebook 中,引流的方式有两种:一种是付费广告;一种是在发布的帖子中直接加入店铺链接。下面主要介绍 Facebook 的付费广告。

（一）Facebook 的广告是什么

简单来说，Facebook 广告实质就是由企业和其他组织在社交网络上建立起来的 Facebook 页面。Facebook 允许广告主根据给定的细分标准划分目标人群，将广告直接送到与他们没有任何关联的用户的 News Feed 中。人们可以对这些广告页面发表评论，并"喜欢（Like）"它们，就像信息流中显示的其他内容一样。如果人们点击"Like"按钮，这些页面将继续显示在他们的信息流中，以及他们的 Facebook"好友"的信息流中。

（二）Facebook 的广告类型

1. 单张图片广告（Single Image）。

广告每次只显示一张图片，但在广告设置时最多可以添加六张不同的图片，以便在展示广告时循环展示。在此种形式中，由于文字比例比较低（20%），所以主要靠图片传递营销信息。像素标准为 1 200×628，标题为 25 个字符，文字为 90 个字符，图片比例为 1.91∶1。单张图片广告示例如图 7-5 所示。

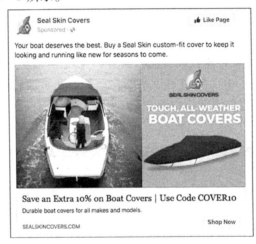

图 7-5 单张图片广告示例

2. 单一视频广告（Single Video）。

单一视频广告只能展示单个视频。视频广告最长可达 60 分钟，最大容量为 2.3 GB，最小分辨率为 720 像素（图 7-6）。

图 7-6 单一视频广告示例

3. 轮播广告（Carousel）。

该广告格式允许用户滚动浏览两个以上不同的图片或视频，视觉效果丰富，广告主可以添加比单个图片广告更多的创意内容。这种广告的文字比例仍然受到20%的约束。每个图片或视频必须是1 080×1 080像素。此种形式适用于在一个广告中展示多个产品或产品版本的情况（图7-7）。

图7-7 轮播广告示例

4. 幻灯片广告。

幻灯片广告是展示产品和讲述品牌故事的绝佳方法，具有抢眼、吸引力强的特点。幻灯片广告制作简单，但吸引力远高于静图广告。与轮播广告类似，幻灯片广告可让用户循环浏览多个广告文案和图片。区别是它们是自动滚动的，而不是靠用户自己。广告主最多可以添加10个视频或图片，最多只能展示50秒，如图7-8所示。

图7-8 幻灯片广告示例

二、Facebook Ads Production Process（脸书广告的制作流程）

（一）创建企业账号

自 2017 年 4 月以来，Facebook 禁止中国大陆地区通过个人广告账户投放广告，个人广告账户投放广告就会被封号。如果想要打广告，就需要开通商业广告账户，商业广告除了通过代理商开通，还可以自行开通。企业账号如图 7-9 所示。

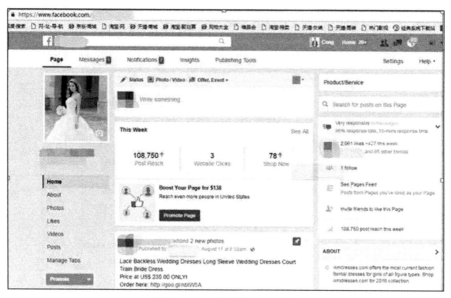

图 7-9　企业账号页面示例

商业页面与个人页面（Personal Profile）的区别：

（1）商业页面更加专业化，有独立的地址，给用户更专业的形象。

（2）可以查看数据详情，及时了解页面粉丝情况。

（3）可以投放广告，更快地推广页面、产品。

（二）定位客户群体

通过对产品客户群体的分析，正确选取受众特征，将产品信息覆盖到潜在客户群体。

（1）可选的受众特征。

可选的受众特征包括居住地、性别、年纪、婚姻及家庭状况、学历、爱好、行为习惯等。

（2）Facebook 收集客户信息的来源主要有以下几种：

- 用户注册信息：出生日期、性别、国籍等。
- 用户内容发送：帖子内容。
- 用户日常行为：赞的页面、加入的群、去过的地方等。

（3）定位客户群体步骤（图 7-10、图 7-11）。

大体上 Preferred Page Audience 在 Facebook 的后台分为以下几类：

- Location.
- Age.
- Gender.

图 7-10　定位客户群体示例（1）

- Interest.
- Languages.
- Behavior.

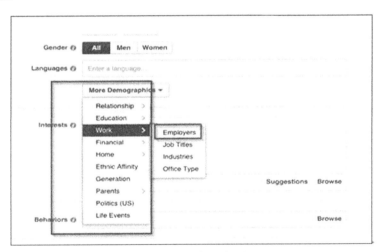

图 7-11　定位客户群体示例（2）

其中的 Interest 又可分为以下几个选项：
- Relationship.
- Education.
- Work.
- Financial.
- Home.
- Ethnic Affinity.

- Generation.
- Parents.
- Politics.
- Life Events.
- Interests.
- Behaviors.

(三) 设置广告预算和投放时间

广告的价格设置，分为每日预算和终身预算两种形式。

每日预算：一段时间内每天的花费。其中最少花费在 5 美元。

终身预算：一段时间内的总花费。

也可以点击高级设置，对广告进行详细的设置，如图 7 – 12 所示。

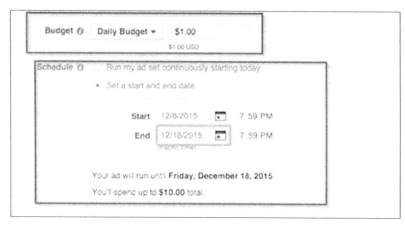

图 7 – 12　设置广告预算和投放时间示例

在正确的时间发表广告，无疑能让更多的人看到。所以，平时发帖时要注意观察，看看在哪一个时段浏览量高。通过大量数据调查，企业在 Facebook 上发文的最佳时间是周四，一天中发文的最佳时间是晚上 8 点。或者可以利用工具，如 Facebook Insight 进行查看（图 7 – 13）哪些帖子在哪个时段是比较受欢迎的。

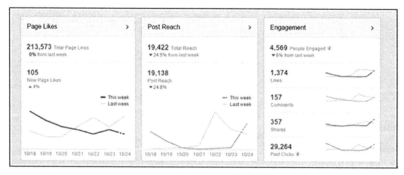

图 7 – 13　Facebook insight 统计示例（1）

(四) 内容创作策略

（1）内容主题：选择客户感兴趣、关心与互动性高的内容。

(2) 内容互动：互动率对信息排名和覆盖人数有很大影响，高互动内容比低互动内容覆盖率高出 5~10 倍及以上。

(3) 内容选取：产品图片、客户使用照片（含好评）、行业热点信息、美图、节日祝贺、视频、促销活动等。

备注：Facebook 对版权要求较低，可以借用一些外来照片做内容发送。文字编辑：2~4 行的文字，问话开头，带出产品特征，结尾带上链接。

（五）广告数据调查

Facebook 广告数据可以通过 Facebook Insight 工具进行查看，在这个工具里主要包含以下几项数据：

- Actions on Page.
- Page Views.
- Page Likes.
- Reach.
- Post Engagement.
- Videos.

通过 Insight 工具提供的数据（图 7-14），运营者可以有针对性地调整广告的设计方案，以更好地满足目标人群的偏好。

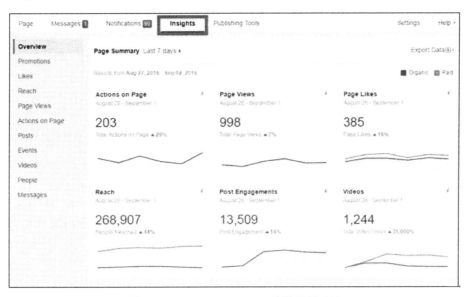

图 7-14　Facebook Insight 统计示例（2）

三、Account Safety（账号安全）

在 Facebook 上做营销，首先要保障自己的账号安全。就像战斗中的根据地，它是我们营销的基地。为了不在冲锋陷阵时老巢被端，请认真看以下几点：

(1) 注册信息中身份证信息一定要真实。

(2) 账号登录地点不要变化，固定 IP 地址。

(3) 加群或者好友不宜过多或者过快。每天被动加好友不超过 200 个，主动加好友不超过 20 个。

（4）不要主动给人发过多信息。

（5）备份好友信息，方便被封号后的验证操作。

Case Study 案例分析

案例 1

一、Watch the Slack Brand AD（欣赏 Slack 品牌图片广告）（图 7 – 15）

图 7 – 15 Slack 品牌图片广告

二、Case Analysis（案例分析）

（一）企业背景

Slack 是一款流行的企业聊天工具，整合了电子邮件、短信、Google Drives、Twitter、Trello、Asana、GitHub 等 65 种工具和服务，可以把各种碎片化的企业沟通和协作集中到一起。

（二）广告文案

标题："Slack：Make Work Better"。

标题通过简单明了的语句点明产品的目标定位。

正文："Slack brings all your communications together in one place."

正文结合职场人的工作情景，提炼产品功能，直戳痛点。

图片文案："What it feels like to sit in 25% fewer meetings."

图片中选择了职场女性作为主角，骑在粉红色木马上，背景搭配彩虹与云朵，给人以梦幻、愉悦、惬意的感觉。用图片带动联想，让目标人群更直观地感受到应用此款软件所带来的工作上的便利与轻松。文案中用数据（25%）让人更加具体地体验到该软件对工作效率的提升空间。使用数据的另一好处是能提升目标人群对企业的信任感。

案例2

一、Watch the Ad of Dollar Shave Club（欣赏 Dollar Shave Club 图片广告）（图 7-16）

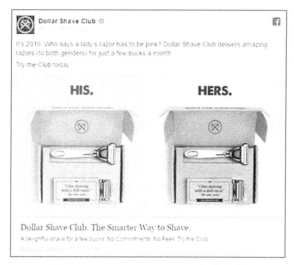

图 7-16　Dollar Shave Club 图片广告

二、Case Analysis（案例分析）

（一）企业背景

Dollar Shave Club 是一个剃须刀品牌，成立于 2012 年 3 月。号称每个月只需 1 美元即可在家享受到剃须产品，这也正是它名称的由来。它的口号是"Shave Money Shave Time"（削减价格，减少时间）。正如它的口号所说的，它旨在为男士减少在剃须刀上的花销和时间。

（二）广告文案

标题："Dollar Shave Club. The Smart Way to Shave"。

Smart 有巧妙的、敏捷的意思，巧妙地用一个词浓缩点明产品卖点。

正文："It's 2016. Who says a lady's razor has to be pink? Dollar Shave Club delivers amazing razors（to both genders）for just a few bucks a month."

开篇用年份（It's 2016）点明新趋势，很明显在刺激追赶潮流的人群。"Who says a lady's razor has to be pink?"反问句的使用，强调了女性的剃刀不一定是粉色的，这从侧面表明了新女性可以和男性是一样的，有力量，能担当。最后一句强化了该品牌的定位——打造实用而低廉的好产品。

这个广告非常聪明，开辟了全新的消费群体——女性。"粉色"刮毛刀既活跃了气氛，又点明了 Dollar Shave Club 产品的目标消费群体。不需生产新的产品，就可以将现有产品线推广到一个巨大的新消费群体。这则广告将 Dollar Shave Club 树立成为紧跟不断变化的社会价值观、具有前瞻性和进取精神的品牌。通过此案例，指导卖家宣传品牌以及将畅销产品推向新的消费群。

Mission Implementation(任务实施)

任务背景：

学习了上述规则之后，Marry 和 Steve 开始着手自己的工作，注册 Facebook 企业账号，为自己的企业网店着手做社交媒体推广。

他们决定根据即将到来的感恩节，为一款彩泥玩具——"彩泥冰激凌机"（图7-17）发布一次单图广告。该产品是幼教博士针对儿童创意启发、身心智能发展设计的，主要针对3~7岁的儿童。该彩泥主要原料为面粉，环保，无味，可重复使用。老板要求这次广告总支出不超过200美元。请参考图7-18、图7-19，按照以下流程帮助 Marry 和 Steve 完成此项任务。

Task 1　Customer Segment（客户分类）

图7-17　彩泥冰激凌机

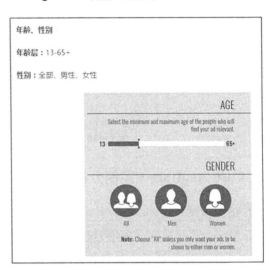

图7-18　目标人群分类参考（1）

图7-19　目标人群分类参考（2）

根据你对产品的判断，目标人群的年龄和性别分别是：

1. Age range：_____, reason：_____.

2. Gender: _____, reason: _____.
3. Parents: _____（只选一项）.
4. Moms: _____（只选一项）.

Task 2　Advertisement Theme（广告主题）

1. Product feature: _____
↓
2. Audience demand: _____
↓
3. Advertisement theme: _____

提示：如何与感恩节联系，并能够切中目标受众痛点。

Task 3　Understand Advertisement Copy（理解广告文案）

单图广告主要靠图片吸引受众，但是文字是点睛之笔。以下对单图广告文字的描述，哪个是正确的？（　　）

A：标题长度为 90 个字符。
B：文字比例占整个广告的 20%。
C：文案只能在图片上方显示。
D：正文长度不能超过 30 个字符。

Task 4　Design Advertisement Copy（设计广告文案）

标题：_____
正文：_____

Task 5　Design Advertisement Picture（设计广告图案）

请对图 7-17 进行一些处理，描述你的创意。
_____（提示：背景、图形元素、文字元素）

Task 6　Advertisement Time and Budget（广告投放时间与预算）

请为该广告设计每日预算以及合适的投放时间：
Start: _____
End: _____
Time: _____ -- _____
Budget (day): _____

Cross-border E-commerce English-Chinese Vocabulary（跨境电商英汉术语对照）

1. facebook	*n.*		脸书
2. twitter	*n.*		推特
3. single image			单图片
4. carousel	*n.*		轮播广告
5. account	*n.*		账户
6. personal	*adj.*		个人的
7. profile	*n.*		侧面；轮廓；外形；剖面；简况

8. segment	n.	一部分，段落
9. audience	n.	观众，受众
10. location	n.	位置
11. gender	n.	年龄
12. interest	n.	兴趣
13. language	n.	语言
14. behavior	n.	行为
15. relationship	n.	关系
16. education	n.	教育
17. financial	adj.	金融的，财政的
18. ethnic	adj.	种族的，部落的
19. affinity	n.	姻亲关系
20. generation	n.	一代人
21. parents	n.	父母
22. politics	n.	政治
23. event	n.	事件
24. budget	n.	预算
25. content	n.	内容
26. strategy	n.	策略
27. data	n.	数据
28. insight	n.	洞察力，洞悉
29. post	n.	帖子
30. engagement	n.	参与度
31. deliver	v.	传递
32. amazing	adj.	令人惊异的
33. buck	n.	（美）钱，元
34. theme	n.	主题
35. advertisement	n.	广告
36. copy	n.	文案
37. customer segment		客户细分

Project 8

Customer Relationship Management(客户关系管理)

Learning Aims(学习目标)

From learning this chapter, students can
1. understand the common method of Customer Relationship Management.
2. understand the goal of Customer Relationship Management.
3. understand the role of "user portrait/customer lags."
4. exercise the ability to understand the core information of Customer Relationship Management.

Lead-in Situation(项目背景)

小熊贸易公司在各个跨境平台的网店已经运营了一段时间,积累了不少顾客信息和数据,但是老板发现客户的复购率还是较低,问题出在哪里呢?老板深知新客户引流需要大量的费用,各种广告、促销活动,以及了解客户的时间成本,然而维持现有老客户的长期关系的成本可以逐年降低,回头客的重复购买会使营运成本降低,随之利润就会提升。老板决定指派客服部 Bullet 专门做客户关系管理工作,以提升老客户的复购率。Bullet 理解老板所说的客户关系管理(CRM)具体是指采用大数据挖掘技术对现有客户进行精准接触、细分、营销、管理和维护。从已有客户信息和网购行为数据中提取出隐藏的、有价值的信息和知识,找出数据中呈现的规律,从而能够解释已知的事实,预测未来的客户行为及业务发展模式,有效辅助店铺运营人员开展精准的营销活动。要想做好这项工作,首先是利用客户数据库做客户标签的开发与应用。

Green-hand Guide(新手指南)

客户标签也称为用户画像,是根据已知的客户信息和已经记录下的客户行为,用一些标签把用户描绘出来,描绘用户的标签就是用户画像(图8-1)。用户画像是对现实世界中用户的数学建模。用户画像的核心是标签体系的建立。标签是某一种用户特征的符号表示,用户画像可以用标签的集合来表示。对于电商或其他实体企业来说,一个很关键的能力就是将客户抽象化,也就是基于用户画像技术的用户信息标签化。把用户的消费层次、行为偏好抽象

8 访客行为分析

在"同一标签化"的层面。这一概念近来演化成一个热门的名词——"同温层",处于该层次的用户是哪一群人、有何共同点,根据这些信息为其提供产品组合,形成一个经济批量的关系,从而改变了传统的单个用户对应单个产品的关系。利用已有用户信息,将用户信息标签化,把共同行为特点、消费层次趋近的用户分到同一消费类别,以期降低企业寻找潜在用户的成本。

图 8-1 用户画像

以 BAT 为代表的电商和互联网公司多年来已经积累了大量的客户数据,这些大数据通常是数量非常巨大的复杂的数据集,用户画像作为大数据的核心组成部分,在电商和互联网公司中具有重要的地位。每一个人都会有自己的基本属性,比如性别、年龄、婚否、收入、教育程度等,每一个电商网站会有一整套的系统来记录用户的行为,比如用户购买行为、浏览行为、点击行为、购物车行为等,可以从这一些行为中判断用户的基本信息,通过这些信息构建出用户画像,进行个性化营销和精准广告投放。

电商企业构建自己的用户画像,最基本和最重要的就是数据收集。一类是静态信息数据,来源于用户注册时所填写的个人资料,或者由此算出的数据。如果有不确定的,可以建立模型来判断,比如用户性别如果不填,根据用户的行为来判断其性别是什么及其概率。典型的静态信息数据有性别、生日、城市、学历、星座、月收入、婚姻状况、职业等。一类是动态信息数据,来源于注册、浏览、点击、购买、签收、评价等用户行为所产生的数据。对于电商来说,购买商品、浏览商品、放入购物车、关注商品是比较重要的行为,根据这些行为就可算出用户注册时间、首单时间、纠结商品、最大消费、退货数量、败家指数、品牌偏好等用户标签(图 8-2)。

每个人在电商平台上浏览和购买的时候,搜索引擎都会给他打上标签(即动态信息数据,又称行为标签)。每个人的行为标签,又可以分成两种:一种是长期行为标签,即定性积累标签。它是大家都能关注到的,在进行个性化自然搜索权重优化的时候都会考虑到的。比如:长期买低端的消费品;长期喜欢韩版风格的东西;注册的时候账号是男性、双鱼座,长期浏览一些花鸟鱼虫类的东西……这一系列的行为都会让网购者形成固定的长期标签,这些标签在其购物、浏览的时候会影响店铺和商品,从而让店铺和商品被打上相应的标签,具备了个性化推荐的基础。另一种是短暂行为标签。比如:你家里刚买了一栋房子,然后你要装修,所以你短期之内购买了墙纸、桌椅、家用电器等,那么搜索引擎就知道了,你这短期的行为爆发暴露了你"买了一栋房子"的行为。所以,这时候什么四件套、水晶吊灯等就

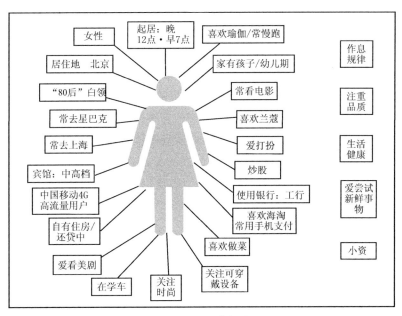

图 8-2 用户标签

开始推荐给你了。如果网店是专卖水晶吊灯的,而且不断地有这种买了房子的人进入该店铺,那么此店铺就会被打上这样的行为标签。

作为跨境电商企业,要想做好客户关系管理的工作以提升业绩,应做到如下三点:

1. 注重客户信息的收集沉淀,形成数据优势,而这种数据优势不应该是数据量的优势,而是将数据转化为有效地服务本企业的技术优势。基于客户分类算法,有效划分客户群体,准确把握客户偏好,将对传统的单个用户跟踪转变为对群体的抽象标签化,进行精准营销。

2. 防范客户信息收集弊病,即只对交易达成的订单有完整的记录,而对订单失败的信息保留不完整甚至无记录等问题,会造成客户数据失衡现象发生。细究,订单失败的信息才应该是企业保留的重要数据,这些信息对企业产品和服务的提升有借鉴作用,并且在产品和服务提升的效果上,这部分数据的影响程度大于订单成功的数据信息。

3. 跨境电商企业在新零售的形势下,应打破线上与线下对立,提高消费体验。以亚马逊为例,为适应消费转型,过去一年新开 140 多家实体书店,而开设实体书店并不是简单回归。亚马逊利用售书积累的数据优势,在实体书店陈列的每本书下面标注网上书评、销售排名,让消费者对该书的销售热度一目了然。

Case Study(案例学习)

客户标签(用户画像)可以用作客户分类统计、营销推荐和数据挖掘。比如,根据用户购买口罩、空气净化剂等防范雾霾的商品数据,与京东平台的星座识别模型相结合,得出了十二星座对雾霾天气的防范指数。敏感的巨蟹座对雾霾防范指数最高,然而挑剔又追求完美的处女座却对雾霾天气的防范指数最低;根据用户的性别,以及购买的一些婴幼儿的产品,经过数据分析得到奶爸当家指数最高的是上海,其次是四川。

各跨境电商平台借助其自身的大数据优势,推出基于客户标签的营销工具,供平台店铺付费使用。"千人千面"就是速卖通、Wish 等平台针对商家推出的店铺商品展示功能模块,是提高转化率的营销工具。根据顾客的特征、需求和行为习惯,在店铺首页为每个人提供个性化的宝贝展示，目的是提高店铺访客转化率。"千人千面"模块功能可以细分子模块，例如："新客热销"模块，重点提高新客户的成交转化率，帮助商家积累沉淀更多的老客户，重点在"新客户"；"潜力新品"模块，重点提高新品的成交转化率，帮助商家快速提高新品成交，重点在"新品"。对每个店铺访客，系统都会根据其个人属性以及其在平台上的实时搜索、浏览、加购、收藏行为，在宝贝库（宝贝库可以由卖家手动设置，也可以由系统根据新客户和新品的场景自动生成）中筛选出当前访客最可能购买的6款宝贝，展示在模块中，所以每个访客看到的宝贝是不一样的，由此实现智能模块级的"千人千面"，可提高访客成交转化率。"千人千面"就是体现跨境电商客户关系管理理念的典型案例。

电商平台是以消费者的购物（浏览）体验作为评价搜索引擎的主要依据。而良好购物体验的主要判断核心是：从消费者产生购物意图到完成购物，花费的时间越短，则购物体验越好。

这也是"千人千面"基于"消费者相互引导论"产生的一个重要原因，而"消费者相互引导论"是怎么产生作用的？下面举例说明：假设 A 买家的客户标签中具备以下三点：性别【女】、年龄【30-35】、消费能力【50-100】。当然，A 买家不仅拥有这些标签，根据平时的浏览习惯和类目的不同，她还同时拥有零零碎碎的各种标签，但只取这三个标签（以下称为 X 标签组）便于分析说明。在 A 买家搜索关键词后，因为买家只拥有三个标签，她的搜索结果出现的产品还是不具备足够的指向性，所以 A 买家的购物时间相对较长，做了一次次的浏览比对款式和价格后，最终她选择 Y 店铺的 Z 产品直接购买（直接购买，即 Z 产品是搜索展现页面中的宝贝；间接购买，即进店后选择同类目的其他产品购买）。

在 A 买家完成下单的这一瞬间，同样拥有 X 标签组的 B 买家、C 买家、D 买家也都同时搜索了这个词，那么系统通过判断（提升购物体验）在综合排序中就会将 Z 产品优先展示给 B、C、D 这些买家。

消费者相互引导论的推荐原则是将相同标签组其他买家的购买结果作为近期展示的判断依据，简单地说就是 Z 产品与 X 标签组买家的契合度高。

因为大类目下的热词搜索产生的转化量非常大，而展现位其实并没有我们想象得那么多（下面会说明），所以"消费者相互引导论"更讲求时效性——"越接近上一次购物的搜索，宝贝就将拥有更多机会的展现"，这其实也是"标签对应论"（宝贝标签、店铺标签与买家标签的契合度）的一种深度解读。在每天大量的优质宝贝的成交中，搜索引擎不会因为某宝贝标签是合适的就优先推荐给买家，即使有推荐也应该是排在近期有成交的宝贝之后的——所以准确地说，"消费者相互引导论""标签对应论"两则理论是同时存在的，而"消费者相互引导论"的优先级又在"标签对应论"之上。

自我诊断：在学习了如上案例后，Bullet 知道，最近店铺流量下降且不稳定、转化率更是低得可怜，是店铺的流量捕捉能力太弱、店内劣质宝贝占比过大造成的影响。关于流量下降问题，要先分析自己的店铺，以前流量多，那流量的端口在哪里，为什么来，又是怎么来的？如果店铺以前有刷单，店铺标签是混乱的，就像之前的 A 买家，她本身与你的契合度很高，但是因为标签对应的原则她是不大可能搜得到你的，而即使 C 买家（和刷手标签对应）通过搜索买了你的宝贝，下一瞬间（同标签相互引导）推荐来的 D 买家也不会下单。如果没有刷单，也没有流量，那只能归因于宝贝详情页、客服购物引导。优秀店铺的搜索转化更好，互相引导的持续性更强（A 转 B，B 转 C，C 转 D……）。

Mission Implementation（任务实施）

阅读下面的材料，并完成文后的任务。

I. Customer Relationship Management

Customer Relationship Management (CRM) is a term that refers to practices, strategies and technologies that companies use to manage and analyze customer interactions and data throughout the customer life-cycle, with the goal of improving business relationships with customers, assisting in customer retention and driving sales growth. CRM systems are designed to compile information on customers across different channels—or points of contact between the customer and the company——which could include the company's website telephone, live chat, direct mails, marketing materials and social media. CRM systems can also give customer-facing staff detailed information on customers' personal information, purchase history, buying preferences and concerns.

According to Bolton, customer satisfaction has significant implications for the economic performances of firms, because it has been found to increase customer loyalty and usage behavior and reduce customer complaints, and the likelihood of customer defection. The complementation of CRM is likely to have an effect on customer satisfaction for at least three reasons: Firstly, firms are able to customize their offerings for each customer. By accumulating information across customer interactions and processing this information to discover hidden patterns, CRM applications help firms customize their offerings to suit the individual tastes of their customers. This customization enhances perceived quality of products and services from a customer's viewpoint, and because perceived quality is a determinant of customer satisfaction, it follows that CRM applications indirectly affect customer satisfaction. Secondly, CRM applications enable firms to provide timely, accurate processing of customer orders and requests and the ongoing management of customer accounts. Thirdly, CRM applications also help firms manage customer relationships more effectively across the stages of relationship initiation, maintenance, and termination.

II. Customer Relationship Management Models

Customer Relationship Management (CRM) involves tracking customers' habits and creating personalized marketing based on customer information that is stored in databases. Most types of customer relationship management models involve information technology, because complex data is an integral part of systems. Types of customer relationship management models include analytic, marketing, customer support, social media, and collaborative databases.

Analytic models collect consumer data at the point of sale and through subsequent interactions such as loyalty programs and consumer surveys. The collected data is used to chart trends and link purchasing habits with customer demographics. Almost all other types of CRM models include some sort of analytic program.

Marketers use CRM information to create demographic-specific promotions and product features. The information helps a marketer track how customers hear about a product, so that he or she can focus on lucrative media channels. Highly customer-specific customer relationship models might tailor promotions and product features for very small markets, which, in some cases, might be only one or two customers.

Specific CRM promotions usually happen only for luxury goods, such as vacation packages or leisure boats. Websites that allow customers to personalize and order products are one form of management models, but the customers themselves input that data and create their products and promotions. Often, companies with these websites will store the customers' information for future CRM and analytical purposes.

Support and service customer relationship management models use stored information to support the product. This type of CRM is often used in the technology and electronics market. When a customer calls for support for a cell phone or a personal computer, the service representative looks up the customer's information using a CRM database. The database lists the product's models and any previous technical issues. This makes support easier for both the tech team and the customer.

Social media is an example of CRM evolving from existing technology. Although social media isn't typical of customer information, on social networks, consumers volunteer everything from demographics to purchasing habits. Public relations specialists and customer support personnel might even interact with consumers using social media platforms.

Collaborative databases have customer information collected by two or more businesses. One company might use this information to sell products to the customers of the other company. Businesses using collaborative databases tend to be in industries that are separate but related.

III. Customer Relationship Management Strategies

Customer Relation Management (CRM) is at the heart of all customer-focused businesses. Repeat business is important to most businesses, and maintaining positive relationships with customers is vital in helping to maximize the amount of business transacted with them. Maintaining good relationships with existing customers is also a form of indirect marketing, as existing customers are then more likely to recommend the business to others.

IV. Tracking customer contacts

An important aspect of CRM is tracking and logging all contacts with customers and prospective customers. The nature and outcome of all contacts should be monitored to identify areas of potential conflicts before they arise, and to understand which contact experiences customers are happy with and which ones may need adjustment. Follow-up calls to customers after any support or service interaction must be sensitively managed, as it is possible to annoy customers by initiating too much customer communication.

V. Staff development

Staff need to be aware at all times of the prevailing business culture regarding customer relationships. A key area to look at is the development of communication skills. This is particularly important in businesses employing technical support staff. It is important that technical staff, who have one-to-one contact with customers at times when customers are experiencing problems, understand the importance of maintaining a positive personal approach in all dealings with customers. Understanding how to resolve the technical issues that the customer may be experiencing is important, but supplying the customer with a positive experience may be the difference in retaining the customer and the customer looking elsewhere in the future. All staff who come into contact with customers or their representatives should receive ongoing training in the development of interpersonal skills. Be sure to let all staff know that every contact with a customer or potential customer is a possible sales contact.

VI. Defining a customer experience strategy

Defining a customer experience strategy involves identifying the level of service the company expects to provide to its customers. For example, a customer experience strategy might include the goal that there must be a response to all customer complaints within a certain time, if the complaint could not be resolved with the initial contact. Another might be to ensure that customers deal with one particular person in the resolution of all issues, or the processing of sales and delivery of goods and services. Staff should be made aware that the defined customer services policy is important to the business, and not an optional set of guidelines. The customer policy must be effectively communicated to all staff at all times, and staff should be encouraged to participate in the development of customer experience strategies, bringing the results of their experience to the process.

Task 1 Look through the text above and complete the following sentences with words or phrases from the box. Change the forms where necessary.

with the goal of	be designed to	at the point of	look...up
at the heart of	be aware of	at all times	be sure to	a set of

1. But he also tells us not to worry but to trust in him _____.
2. I _____ your address _____ in the personnel file.
3. That, after all, is how our political system _____ work.
4. That personal link is _____ blogging.
5. Suddenly you find yourself _____ no return.
6. It means maintaining an active interest in the person _____ ensuring their success.
7. He has turned _____ chair legs.
8. Technological progress _____ supply the necessary components.
9. They should _____ their rights.

Task 2 Translate the following sentences into Chinese.

1. Customer Relationship Management (CRM) is a term that refers to practices, strategies and technologies that companies use to manage and analyze customer interactions and data throughout the customer life-cycle, with the goal of improving business relationships with customers, assisting in customer retention and driving sales growth.

2. By accumulating information across customer interactions and processing this information to discover Hidden patterns, CRM applications help firms customize their offerings to suit the individual tastes of their customers.

3. Highly customer-specific customer relationship management models might tailor promotions and product features for very small markets, which, in some cases, might be only one or two customers.

4. When a customer calls for support for a cell phone or a personal computer, the service representative looks up the customer's information using a CRM database.

5. Although social media isn't typical of customer relationship management models, the websites can be viewed as interactive databases full of customer information.

Task 3　Read the text again and arrange the statements in a proper order.

1. By accumulating information across customer interactions and processing this information to discover hidden patterns, CRM applications help firms customize their offerings to suit the individual tastes of their customers. (　　)

2. CRM systems can also give customer-facing staff detailed information on customers' personal information, purchase history, buying preferences and concerns. (　　)

3. Another might be to ensure that customers deal with one particular person in the resolution of all issues, or the processing of sales and delivery of goods and services. (　　)

4. Staff needs to be aware at all times of the prevailing business culture regarding customer relationships. (　　)

5. Highly customer-specific customer relationship management models might tailor promotions and product features for very small markets, which, in some cases, might be only one or two customers. (　　)

6. Customer Relationship Management (CRM) involves tracking customers' habits and creating personalized marketing based on customer information that is stored in databases. (　　)

7. This type of CRM is often used in the technology and electronics market. (　　)

Cross-border E-commerce English-Chinese Vocabulary （跨境电商英汉术语对照）

1. user profile		用户画像
2. user portrait		用户画像
3. personas	n.	用户画像
4. Artificial Intelligence (AI)		人工智能
5. big data		大数据
6. cloud computing		云计算
7. data mining		数据挖掘
8. push	n. & v.	推送
9. Customer Relationship Management		客户关系管理
10. customer satisfaction		客户满意
11. customer defection		客户流失
12. social network		社交网络